Spiritual Awakenings II

More Journeys of the Spirit
From AA Grapevine

AAGRAPEVINE, Inc.
New York, New York
www.aagrapevine.org

D0187547

"The greatest gift that can
come to anybody
is a spiritual awakening."

Bill W.
AA Grapevine, December 1957

AA Preamble

Alcoholics Anonymous is a fellowship of men and women
who share their experience, strength and hope
with each other that they may solve their common problem
and help others to recover from alcoholism.

The only requirement for membership is a desire to stop drinking.
There are no dues or fees for AA membership;
we are self-supporting through our own contributions.
AA is not allied with any sect, denomination, politics, organization
or institution; does not wish to engage in any controversy,
neither endorses nor opposes any causes.

Our primary purpose is to stay sober
and help other alcoholics to achieve sobriety.

©AA Grapevine, Inc.

Contents

SECTION THREE
Miracles, Mysteries, Synchronicities

SECTION FOUR
AA's Big Hoop

Welcome

As usual, our AA co-founder Bill W. did not mince words when writing about the subject of this book. With his own white light experience one of the classics of written history, he referred to a spiritual awakening as "the greatest gift that can come to anybody," but he also made it clear that a spiritual awakening is not just a lovely possibility, not merely an option. In the December 1957 issue of AA Grapevine he put it this way:

"We must awake or we die.

"So we do awake, and we are sober. Then what? Is sobriety all that we are to expect of a spiritual awakening? Again, the voice of AA speaks up. No, sobriety is only a bare beginning, it is only the first gift of the first awakening ... a new life of endless possibilities can be lived if we are willing to continue our awakening."

It is commonly acknowledged that we drank in a futile search for spirit, so it's no surprise that alcohol also goes by the name of "spirits," with some package stores even named "spirit shops." But alcohol took away our spirits, and it's only when we find the real thing through the liberating program of Alcoholics Anonymous that we realize we have come home.

Let one of the writers in this book describe what that feels like:

"You, too, can live—really live. There will be love and laughter and a delicious sense of well-being down deep inside if you will abandon yourself to the business of recovery—not just recovery from the disease of active alcoholism, but deeper than that, recovery from a former self. Such thorough recovery can be realized, I believe, only through the fearless application of spiritual principles to our daily lives."

Written by men and women made new in spirit, these are stories that will light our way home.

SECTION ONE

A Daily Reprieve

Alcoholics may be granted, as we are told in our literature, not a cure, but a temporary reprieve, contingent on our spiritual condition.

Funny about that word "reprieve." Official definitions range from an offhand "to give relief for a time" to the more chilling "a temporary suspension of the execution of a sentence, esp. of death."

A death sentence. This is always a shock to read, yet all of us who have suffered, who have seen others die at the hands of our rapacious creditor, know how dangerous it is to shrink from that reality—our reality. We are spared daily, however, given twenty-four hours worth of grace, most often by doing a few significant things and joining others at our simple gatherings.

These are stories of power only gained by acknowledging our powerlessness. "I felt myself move with a new power, courage, and faith that, by the grace of God, I have acquired as a result of working the Twelve Steps of Alcoholics Anonymous," says one alcoholic, as she finds the courage to make financial amends to the government. Here's a man on the run, twelfth-stepped by a cab driver, another who found his wife in AA on Thanksgiving, another who only started drinking when he lost his wife, and a woman who drank to celebrate her decision to go with "AA all the way!"

Here's an inmate who woke up from drinking shaving lotion to cry, "Lord God, if you are there, take this life of mine and run it." Here's a woman who, after twelve years of sobriety, is still looking outside of herself for a reward. "Meditation has become a daily gift of self-love," a former inmate reports. And more than one of us has found great cyber-fellowship: "The greetings and cheerfulness on the screen made me feel safe," one young girl says.

Enjoy these stories of spiritual reprieve, as varied, colorful—and powerful— as what takes place in our precious "rooms of AA."

Life and Taxes

June 2005

L ast November, I began working the Steps in order to take responsibility for my past—and especially to make amends to the Internal Revenue Service for twenty-three years of failing to file income tax returns. Yesterday, I signed, sealed, and mailed the final four years of my taxes. I went to my accountant, with a conscious contact of my Higher Power, ready to take whatever was coming to me. I felt myself move with a new power, courage, and faith that, by the grace of God, I have acquired as a result of working the Twelve Steps of Alcoholics Anonymous.

The attorneys tell me that I am open to possible criminal charges. The accountants tell me that the government may say I owe up to thirty thousand dollars more in back taxes. And yet, at this moment, I am at ease. There are no fears or anxieties, no doubts or insecurities, and no trepidation about what might happen in the future.

Furthermore, I'm not judging myself for being irresponsible. I am simply doing this with an attitude of self-compassion, kind of what I imagine a loving parent would feel toward a child who just wasn't able to do any better at the time. It's a big step for a fellow who had lost all faith in God and his life.

The malignant doubt that had poisoned my life for forty-two years (including ten years of sobriety) is gone, thanks to God and the AA program. I am incredibly happy and joyous, and free of the restless, irritable, and discontented life I used to know. I only want to do God's will to the best of my ability. And each day, my life just gets better and better.

J.B.
Connecticut

The Fugitives

May 2004

My wife and I stood before the federal judge and listened to her pronounce sentence on us. We were both going to do prison time. We'd been through a lot in the twenty years we'd been together. We'd drunk and drugged together, and now we were both going to prison on a drug-dealing charge. I like to say that we were "codependents and codefendants."

How had I gotten here? I had certainly come a long way from the fifteen-year-old who'd hung out with the older guys because they could buy booze for me. I remember that I always drank more than my friends and could never seem to get enough. In college, I started drinking every night, and the only way I would wake up to get to class was by setting up a device with my stick that would knock over a huge pyramid of beer cans when my alarm clock went off. As the beer cans came crashing down, I would drag myself out of my stupor and head to class.

Some years later, I had a job working as an all-night country and western disc jockey. My shift would start at midnight and I would drink right up until 11:45 P.M. and then make a mad dash to the radio station. The guy I relieved would put on a long record for me, and I would fall into the chair trying to pull myself together. I would sober up by about 6:00 A.M. at the end of my shift. I can't imagine what I must have sounded like to the audience and was not very surprised when I got fired.

At another point, my wife and I were living on a fifty-seven-foot boat in New York City and would order our booze by the case from the neighborhood liquor store. Because we lived on a large boat, the liquor store thought we entertained a lot, but it was just the two of us drinking alone and drinking unbelievable quantities of booze. We had been dancing for a lot of years, and now we were going to have to pay the piper.

After sentencing us, the judge said that we were to be given a "voluntary surrender." That meant we had three weeks to get our affairs in order before we had to report to our respective prisons. I hadn't been able to get my affairs in order for forty years, so I had no idea how I was going to do it now. But I was going to have to go whether my affairs were in order or not. Most of the three weeks were consumed with getting the alcohol and drugs we were convinced we needed to survive. The day came to go, but we didn't know how we could live without our alcohol and drugs. So we chose to pursue them instead of showing up at prison.

Now we were on the run; we were hunted fugitives. We found ourselves living in an abandoned apartment; I went out stealing all day so we could buy what we needed. I remember waking up in the morning and saying, "Not another day of this. I can't do this any more." Then I'd get up and go out and start all over again. I had reached the jumping off place that the Big Book talks about. I could not live with alcohol or without it. I had no idea how to get off the hamster wheel I was on, so I just kept running.

In the next couple of weeks, several incidents took place that seemed unrelated and just fortunate coincidences. In retrospect, I know that God was giving me all the rope I needed. We were living in New York City, and we decided it would be safer if we got out of town. We ended up in a cheap motel in a small town in upstate New York, a few hours from the city. My wife was pretty drunk one night and decided at 2:00 A.M. that she was going to go out and get some food. Somehow she managed to drive down the road about a mile to an all-night diner. As she was leaving the diner, a New York State trooper observed her car weaving and pulled her over. Her driver's license indicated that she was from New York City and her past experience had told her that New York State troopers are not overly fond of people from the city. He gave her a breathalyzer test, which showed she was more than legally drunk. She knew that this was the end and we had finally been caught. She sat there waiting for the inevitable as the trooper called in her license on the radio.

Suddenly, the trooper appeared at her window once more and handed back her license. He then pointed her in the right direction and told her to drive carefully. She couldn't believe what was happening, but she didn't stop to ask questions; she just got out of there as fast as she could. By all rights, we should have been arrested right then, but God felt we weren't quite ready and still needed more rope.

We counted ourselves lucky and immediately left upstate New York. We decided we would be better off back in the city where we wouldn't stick out so much. About a week later, I found myself in an area of New York's Lower East Side nicknamed "Alphabet City" because the avenue names are letters of the alphabet—Avenue A, Avenue B, Avenue C. The further down the alphabet you go, the tougher the neighborhood gets. I was there to buy drugs. Normally, the police don't bother you there much, but that day they were doing one of their semiannual sweeps. I was arrested and taken to the Manhattan Criminal Courts building. I found myself lying on the floor of the jail cell, miserable and sick. Although I had given them a phony name, they took my fingerprints. I figured it was only a matter of time before they found out I was wanted by the Feds. But being caught wasn't on my mind. The only thing I could think about was how I was going to get through the night with nothing to ease the pain.

The following morning, in a semidazed state, I was led through court and told by a court-appointed lawyer that if I would plead guilty they'd let me out for time served. Sounded like a deal to me and before I knew it, I was back on the street. I couldn't believe that they hadn't caught me. But God knew I wasn't ready and needed just a little more rope.

A week later, my wife and I were back down in Alphabet City. We took a cab downtown and my wife held the cab on the corner while I went to buy what we needed. I got back into the cab with fifteen bags of dope in my pocket, and the cab driver suddenly turned around and looked directly at us. He said, "I was a slave to alcohol and drugs for twenty-five years, but I don't have to live like that any more because I have God in my life." Oh great, I thought. This is just what I need. I can't wait to get back to do my dope, and this guy wants to talk about God. Then he looked right at us and asked, "Do you two want to stop?" and without a moment's hesitation we both said yes. He said, "Then let's join hands and pray and ask God to help you stop."

Now, when I had prayed before, I said something like, "Oh God, please make sure my contacts are there," or "Oh God, please make sure he's got the stuff." In fact, I'd often asked God to help me stay sick. I'd never thought of asking him to help me get well. Now the time was right. God had finally given me enough rope, and I was at the end of it. There in the back seat of that taxicab, with fifteen bags of dope in my pocket, holding hands with this cab driver whose name I didn't even know, I sincerely asked God to help me stop. I had finally surrendered.

The very next morning, we were picked up by the federal marshals and taken away to start our prison sentences. Although I didn't know it at the time, this was the answer to my prayer. That was the last time I had a drink or a drug in what is now almost eighteen years.

The two and half years that I spent in prison were a wonderful experience for me. It was there that I found Alcoholics Anonymous, the Twelve Steps, and a God of my understanding. It was there in prison, using the Steps, that I started to take responsibility for my life. For the first time, I was learning to like myself.

The principles of Alcoholics Anonymous that I learned in prison and after I got out still guide my daily life. For my wife and me, Alcoholics Anonymous is the center of our lives. We are both active in corrections work, sharing our stories with those who are still incarcerated, and the message we bring to them is one of hope. We sponsor newcomers and do service at several different levels. It seems the more I give to Alcoholics Anonymous, the better my life gets.

Today I have an incredible life in Alcoholics Anonymous. I have a beauti-

ful family, run a successful business of my own, and am a useful and productive member of my community. Best of all, my life has meaning today. Alcoholics
Anonymous has given me something of real value that I can share with others. I
get to see God's grace changing their lives just as it did mine.

Dennis W.
Tucson, Arizona

Mama Tried

July 2006

I discovered alcohol at the age of thirteen, then drank as much as I could, as
fast as I could, for the next ten years.

I can't stop drinking once I start. So during that time, I found myself in
jails in six different states and one intensive care unit, where I almost died of
alcohol poisoning at fifteen. They were all alcohol-related incidents.

Before I graduated from high school, I'd wrecked four cars. I drove one
into the side of a factory in my hometown of Newton, Iowa. My nickname was
"Crash."

A month after I graduated, I decided to appease my father by joining the
Navy to "become a man." My twenty-eight-month naval career helped introduce
me to four of the six states mentioned earlier.

One evening, on the USS Enterprise, I heard someone asking for me. I
turned around to see two Masters-At-Arms. They took me into custody and I was
charged with possession and distribution of a controlled substance. The court-
martial took place when we returned to port in Alameda, California.

I was convicted and celebrated my twentieth birthday in the brig at a place
called Treasure Island. In Merle Haggard's song, "Mama Tried," the lyrics say, I
turned twenty-one in prison/doing life without parole/And there's no one for me
to blame/'cuz Mama tried. God bless my mom. She had tried!

Give an alcoholic enough rope, and he'll eventually hang himself. While I
awaited discharge, I was caught getting high one night in the barracks.

"You're a drunk, a dope fiend, and a loser," the commander shouted the next morning, "and I don't want you in my Navy!" Her daddy was an admiral and she meant it.

I was used to that sort of reaction. My own dad had "kicked me out of the
family" for being court-martialed. I had sullied his name for the last time. (Today,
thanks to AA, we have a peaceable relationship.)

I lasted three more years "out there." At one point I even moved to Austin, Texas, in an attempt to find my birth mother (I'm an adoptee). If I just find my roots, I

won't be such a drunk, I thought. Thank God, I didn't find her at that time.

I came into the rooms for good on an October night in 1987. Stewart, a man who would become my sponsor, invited me to coffee, knowing I was sick and angry. Later, as he drove me to my apartment on Alcatraz Avenue (I'm not kidding), he pointed something out to me that I hope I never forget.

"You know, Larry, it doesn't take a genius to walk out onto their back porch, look up at the stars, and snap to the fact that you, I, or any other human being could not have made all this." I flashed on a starlit night from my childhood, riding with my parents in our Impala. I felt as if everything was happening very quickly and slowly at the same time. I didn't know what it meant at the time, but had held it in my mind until Stewart said those words.

I laughed in response, and I had not laughed in a very long time. Next day, I asked him to be my sponsor. He said yes and gave me the flashlight and road map to work the Twelve Steps of Alcoholics Anonymous.

Alcoholics Anonymous got my attention with the disease concept. All of my drinking life I had been told that I was a drunk and a loser. From the beginning, I accepted my inability to stop drinking once I started. I didn't know my body was physiologically different until I came to AA and heard about the physical allergy, coupled with the mental obsession. Without doubt, this concept saved my life. There's no shame in it.

Which leads me back to my time in the brig at Treasure Island. At different times in my sobriety, I have served as meeting secretary, coffee maker, general service representative, intergroup representative, and been on Hospitals and Institutions (H&I) committees. I believe in one alcoholic, one service commitment.

So, when a guy from H&I said he was going to "TI," I leapt at the chance to go with him.

My sponsor suggested I wait until I was one year sober and had gone through the Steps before I tried to find my birth mother. I did as he suggested and found her in Austin when I was three years sober, along with the paternal side of my biological family. I met my paternal grandfather shortly after he was paroled after serving twenty years in a Texas maximum-security prison. He died not long after.

On a subsequent visit to Austin, I mentioned him to an old-timer after a meeting. The old-timer replied, "I met your granddad once about twenty years ago, when I took an H & I meeting into Huntsville." I walked out into the parking lot and bawled. I never knew my grandfather had a taste of AA, and it puzzled me why sobriety had been given to me. But, as granddad said when we met, "I don't need a paternity test to tell you're my grandchild." Right back at ya, Granddad.

In my fifth year of sobriety, I lived in a monastery in Big Sur, California, working for a famous monk as his liaison. The Rule of St. Benedict states, "Sit in your cell, as in paradise." Thanks to living one day at a time in AA, I can go anywhere, provided it is on my Father's business, and have access to paradise.

Today, I have a beautiful wife who I met in AA on a Thanksgiving morning, a son, and countless friends, as well as eternal gratitude.

Thank you, AA, for reaffirming my desire to not drink today.

Larry K.F.
Studio City, California

In Search of the Secret

May 1997

On joining AA, I was struck by the jovial mood of the members and wanted to know their secret. I grabbed the Big Book, the Grapevine, and the new Step book, *Twelve Steps and Twelve Traditions*, in a desperate attempt to stay sober. I had forfeited my business, my home, and my family—including my two daughters—in one fell swoop.

Following a youth during which my drinking was controlled by the Depression came a tour with the RCAF in World War II, in areas where booze was not always available. I was then discharged to a depleted world. I was in a drained and restless mood, and alcohol became a way of life. I found nothing in common with civilians and was bored in their company, but I did find a job, get married, and try my hand at settling down. I pushed baby carriages and moved through two jobs. Then I tried real estate selling, where my time was my own, and the time clock didn't interfere with my drinking.

With my marriage on the rocks, I visited a psychiatrist who told me to pick a new vocation, start from the bottom, work up in business, and win back my family. Booze became a real handicap now, and although I had a lot of will power and determination, I found myself straining at the bit. When the tension became intolerable, I'd turn to drink, thinking that preferable to going bananas. This trend continued until my drinking threatened my new job, which required punching a clock but paid well and offered a good pension on retirement.

As a new employee, I was required to work that first Christmas Day. My buddies of the night before dumped me onto a bus to go to work. Then my hangover hit me, and I found myself at the end of the bus line, although I'd told the driver where to let me off. He took me back, and I awoke at the start of the line. I guess the driver was hungover too.

From then on booze took over, but I wanted to hold on to this job, and through sheer determination, plugged on. Then I went on the drunk to end all drunks. This one was different somehow. I just couldn't get loaded, and the fact came home that I could no longer drown my troubles, which scared the daylights out of me. Then I went for a walk in the downtown area of the city.

Suddenly I came up short. Booze!—that was my problem. In a flash of clarity, I saw that if I could beat this curse, I could recover. But how? I remembered a questionnaire I'd done in our local paper, but which I'd rejected as extreme, although it appeared to hit the mark in a number of areas. Perhaps AA was the answer after all. Going into a phone booth, I found a group listed nearby, which I entered at 4:00 p.m. and by God's grace was open. I realized later that given another few hours of reflection I could have had a change of heart, so unstable was I at this point. For an instant hope inspired my determination to give this last resort one hell of a try.

The first weeks were crucial. To still my inner turmoil I studied the Big Book—"Bill's Story," "We Agnostics," and the basic action Step, the Third Step. One night, in a state of near delirium, I concentrated on the paragraph that contains the Third Step prayer. Feeling highly elated, I went to sleep.

In the middle of the night I awoke in a sweat. Was I never to take another drink for the rest of my life—that elixir that seemingly had brought me through so many scrapes? The idea shocked me! Then I remembered that all I had to do is to stay sober one day at a time. Again, I fell asleep and the compulsion to drink was lifted from me and was never to reoccur. The test came two weeks later.

I was working on some real estate I owned, in July, the hottest time of the year. My thirst was overpowering. I choked on a soda pop, and being convinced that beer was the only drink to assuage, I threw my tools into the car and hightailed it to the coolest bar in town, which was a shaded float over the river. At the bridge I stopped with the crushing realization that I was now in AA and understood the importance of the first drink. What to do?

With my heart in my hands, I said a prayer. Visions of another debauchery crept in, and the horror of working in the clutches of another hangover flooded my thoughts. I drove home and made a cup of tea and lay down. That battle was over. I knew it would have taken an all-night drinking session to still my craving if I had capitulated to that first drink.

A few months later, I got drunk to give me the nerve to sever a relationship. That was my last drink. In my first years in AA I was burdened by not being able to reconcile my marriage, as others appeared to have done. But the Twelve Steps enabled me to transcend the trauma, and I was able to hold my job and maintain my two daughters, who on maturity came to live with me, while my ex-wife passed away later without seeing the light. In my four-score years, one half in

AA, I've found myself a survivor. I have the respect of my family and the church I joined after my awakening. In the spiritual aspects of AA I can find unlimited opportunities to round out my retirement years.

I believe that AA should be recognized at the close of this millennium, as the most progressive health advance of the twentieth century. In my opinion it has saved more lives than all the antidepressants and painkillers churned out by our geniuses in pharmacy and psychiatry.

My gratitude goes out to Bill W. and Dr. Bob for this remarkable Fellowship, and to Lois and Anne for sticking with their spouses through their shaky quest to alleviate lonely suffering and conciliate fragile families.

George V.
Winnipeg, Manitoba

Someone's Got to Show the Way

May 1959

One of the swellest guys I ever met was Tom. I find myself thinking about him often because he's my idea of a man, and because his story is a departure from the run-of-the-mill type of drunk. Tom never got drunk in his life until he was fifty-six years old. That's when his wife died. He and the missus were a devoted couple and their lives were wrapped up in each other because they'd never had any children.

Almost overnight she took sick and was gone, and Tom was left stricken and bewildered. Tom was a steady-plugging gentle type of person and he and mama had a love so deep for each other they had no need for a real, personal love of God. So, when his wife passed away, Tom had no one to turn to for comfort.

For a while he spent most of his time hunched over a freshly risen mound at the cemetery wishing he were down there with her. Life wasn't worth living and he walked about like a zombie, seeing nothing, hearing nothing, feeling nothing but the raw spot in his heart. He just wanted to die because he couldn't think of any reason to live.

He wandered into a bar one day and never came out, he said, until two-and-a-half years later—and only then because his money and credit gave out. Never worked a stroke the whole time. He had turned bitter on life and claimed he was the most miserable man alive, hating everyone in particular and the world in general.

He'd spent his savings, sold his home and converted everything he owned that was salable into cash. There he drank it up bottle by bottle. Six years later he was a withered wreck of a man, shaking out a bout with the dts in the alcoholic ward of a city hospital.

There was a resident doctor there who had been working with AA and knew his drunks well. He had Tom on paraldehyde as he brought him through the DTs. Pretty soon Tom was crying for his medicine like a baby crying for its bottle. The doctor shut him off, but finally agreed to give him a little if he'd talk to a couple of guys from AA. Tom would do anything. Well, the guys came to visit two or three times a day but they couldn't get through to him because he was living in another world. As a last resort they gave Tom a kind of shock treatment—accused him of being a quitter and told him the facts of life in no uncertain terms. Tom came up out of bed and raved like a madman. The guys left. Sometime during the night something of what the men said got through to Tom. Next morning he lay quiet and attentive, listening to what his visitors said.

Tom had been sober five years when I met him at Men's Town, after hearing him talk to a bunch of drunks sent there by judges in the surrounding towns. What a man—alive to his fingertips, bursting with energy and a zest for living that would put to shame a doddering teenager. When he listended to a man's problems he crooned and clucked in genuine understanding, his eyelids veiled with the heavy film of compassion.

Tom picked the toughest cookies of them all and the drunks he pulled back from the lip of hell would fill a city square. I'll bet his wife is beaming proudly somewhere up there to watch the likes of Tom as he lives each day to the fullest, giving everything he's got, piling up treasure in heaven that will take eternity to spend. You could tell by the look in his eye he had a new love, a love that would never fail.

It is assuring to know there are men like Tom in the world, lighting a candle here and there, cutting a swath through the darkness. Someone's got to show the way, and it's guys like Tom who'll be doing it.

G.L.
Boise, Idaho

There Can Be Love and Laughter

February 1974

On June 8, 1961, while sitting in a boat fishing a picturesque little lake in Illinois, I reached a decision. I had returned to the scenes of my childhood to visit my mother, and for one week I had come daily to this tranquil spot to fish, to pray and meditate, and to reflect back over the years of my life as an active alcoholic.

There had been a brief interlude of dryness, when I was going to AA meetings for a period of three months. But then had come the old call of the wild, and I had bolted, rejoining the pack—the old cronies in their dens.

Now I was at the turning point. What was I to do about my life and the influence my life was having on those around me? The choice was mine to make. Was I to continue down the path of self-willed destruction, filled with hangovers, remorse, confusion, and chaos, or was I to stop, make an about-face, and follow the AA path with God and his people as my guides?

It was not a decision made lightly, I agonized over the emptiness of life without all my good drinking friends. Where would love and romance come from? Love and romance were important to me. Where would laughter and fun come from? Laughter and fun were important to me. God didn't like gaiety, I rationalized. God frowned on frivolity. The church of my parents had said so. Was I capable of living out my allotted time in solemn, somber sobriety?

My mind flooded with memories of the price I had always paid for the fleeting gaiety, the hollow laughter, the pseudo loves. I made the decision. "Okay, God. You win. It's AA all the way—starting tomorrow."

That's the way it was. The decision, I mean.

I pulled anchor, steered my little boat landward, and never looked back at the tranquil spot, the tiny cove with its tree-filled shores, its quietness and majestic calmness.

Heading to the nearest bar to celebrate my decision, I drank the rest of the day, while driving back to my home in Northern Indiana.

The next morning, June 9, 1961, there was a note of finality to that hangover. I had drained the last dregs from the cup. I had had enough. It was finished.

That was thirteen years ago, and each morning since that day, when I have awakened, I have had the feeling "I have had enough."

Let me tell you about my mornings now. Upon awakening, I take my cup of coffee to the patio of our small, pink house nestled under great oaks and hickory trees along the shoreline of a tranquil cove on a picturesque lake in Illinois. Soon, my husband joins me. My husband—the first boy I ever loved, the idol of my high-school days, returned to me through the divine grace of the Higher Power I came to know through a program of Steps to recovery. We have our morning prayers and meditation in harmony with the birds and God's little critters scampering about.

My gaze fixes on a spot out in the cove. I see a woman in a small boat. I feel again her loneliness, her fears and frustrations. I hurt for her; but there is a sweetness to the pain, the sweetness of gratitude, for she lives only in my memories. May she always abide there. I have gone full circle, returning now to the exact location where I made the weighty decision that changed my life.

I write now to that new woman—and to any woman new in our Fellowship today. That lonely, fearful woman, who cannot envision life without alcohol and all the familiar ramifications of a drinker's life. Thirteen years ago, forty years old, twice divorced, all I could see stretching ahead was an empty path for me to trudge alone.

Go to work; come home; meet the family's needs; go to AA meetings alone; come home alone; go to bed alone. Do the best I could about an inventory of self. Relate the sordid details of a seemingly wasted life to another human being. Make humble petitions for forgiveness to those I had harmed. Each morning, day after day after day, ask the God of my limited understanding for his guidance "today." Some days, almost hourly, renew the plea for his way in my life.

But, ever so slowly, I could feel myself changing. Things that had seemed important were no longer important. There was inside me a warming, a softening, a stirring, as the petals of a rosebud stir almost imperceptibly into a blossom.

You, too, can live, new woman—really live. There will be love and laughter and a delicious sense of well-being down deep inside if you will abandon yourself to the business of recovery—not just recovery from the disease of active alcoholism, but deeper than that, recovery from a former self. Such thorough recovery can be realized, I believe, only through the fearless application of spiritual principles to our daily lives.

I hear the katydids, the buzz of the locusts, and I am reminded of a passage I read about a man named Joel. The locusts had devastated his lands year after year, but God said to Joel, "I will restore to you the years the locusts have taken."

My heart swells and tears of gratitude fill my eyes, for I, too, have had restored to me the years of the locusts, through a blessed fellowship called AA.

Alcoholics Anonymous is a fellowship of men and women who share. Thank you, Grapevine, for letting me share.

N. G.
Neoga, Illinois

Close Shave

December 1998

I n the fall of 1971, I was on my usual holiday drunk. It was the kind where I appreciated being able to go to a bar and not feel uncomfortable because I was shaking and looked like warmed-over death. A simple statement to the barkeep—"I really hung one on last night"—was enough to get a little sympathy and a double Bloody Mary. After about six o'clock, I'd start to get the eye, and it would be time to leave, but I was all right now.

After upsetting Thanksgiving dinner for my beloved wife and beautiful little daughter, I promised I would go to the basement rec room and get myself straight and give them a good Christmas. I lay on the couch with my wine bottles to help me taper off and went out the back door once a day to get more wine and a fast-food dinner or such. Occasionally, my wife would stick her head down the stairs to see if I was still alive. After a couple of weeks of this, I started the usual process of not being able to sleep; I was shaking and puking. I tried drinking nothing but sherry wine very slowly and sipping warm beer but nothing would stay down. I knew if I could just get a little alcohol in my system I would stop hurting so much. Nothing seemed to work. As fast as it would go down it would come back up.

Sometime on the eighteenth of December, I apparently became psychotic and took a 32-caliber pistol and put a bullet into my right temple. It is probably the grace of God that I don't remember it, and an even greater grace that my wife and daughter were out doing some Christmas shopping. When they got home they found me with what appeared to be a scalp wound, so 911 was called. The exit wound was hidden by my thick hair. While in intensive care, the pressure in my head started building up and I was rushed to the operating room for emergency surgery. I was in a coma for almost a week. When my wife asked the doctor what the chances of my surviving were, he said I had a thirty percent chance—if I regained consciousness. When asked what the quality of my life would be, the doctors wouldn't even discuss it. I finally regained consciousness on Christmas Day.

For twenty-five years I've tried to find the words to express the emotional and physical pain that I felt that day. What does a drunk do when he hurts and wants a drink? I didn't have anyone I could call to bring me something to drink and I had no money. But my wife had left my shaving kit with a bottle of shaving lotion in it. Don't scoff unless you've tried it. Two fingers of shaving lotion and four fingers of water and it will make up milky white, and it will do the job. Next, I needed to figure out how to get some more. I decided I could break the shaving lotion bottle and then I'd be given another one. If you want to break a shaving lotion bottle, you'd better get a sledgehammer. I banged it on the metal side of the bed and on the floor until I was exhausted. Finally, in sheer disgust, I threw it on the floor with all my strength. It hit the floor, bounced up to the ceiling and come down on some metal hospital chairs. One big racket! Since I was directly across from the nurses' station, they all came running. "What happened?" Nothing, I just dropped my shaving lotion bottle.

Somehow, this is what it took for me to be reduced to the point of hopelessness and helplessness. In disgust and desperation I lay back on my pillow and cried into the darkness. "Lord God, if you are there, take this life of mine and run it." I knew nobody could make a worse mess of it than me. This is probably the only time in my life that I've been totally devoid of any ego. As I lay there, I began to realize that every time I'd been in trouble I'd been drinking. Every time I'd wrecked a car, been in jail, been in a psycho ward—I'd been drinking. Unbeliev-able. If I didn't drink I didn't get in trouble. Not that every time I drank, I got in trouble—in my youth I had a whole lot of fun. But somewhere along the line the gadget broke. And I spent years trying to fix it, to no avail.

Little did I realize that I had just taken the first three Steps of AA without reservation.

Some get this program easily, but for some of us we have to go the hard way. Now, after all these years, I am the most blessed man alive. In spite of the fact that doctors cannot find the right medication to control the seizures, the loss of balance, and the sleep apnea, I've had the opportunity to give my wife and daughter that good Christmas I promised them. And I've had the chance to be the loyal, faithful, and loving husband to the best of my ability, and a real father. Through many years of carrying this message to the local jail, I've had the joy of seeing several men really put their lives back together and become productive, law-abiding sober citizens. Not my works but God made them responsive to the message. Thank God and this program, which makes it all so simple. If I do not drink, I do not get in trouble!

Anonymous
Fairfax, Virginia

Where's My Reward?

September 2005

This coming October will mark my twelfth year of sobriety, but even with the passage of time, the inner demons of the alcoholic mind don't roll over and die that easily.

As my AA birthday draws near, a lot of old stuff has been coming up, a lot of thoughts and feelings that I associate with my alcoholic identity. There's a mindset around drinking that still haunts me from time to time, and that's the whole "reward" aspect. I so clearly remember being twenty-four years old and driving home from my receptionist job over the canyon on a Friday night think-ing, Yep, I put in a good week and now it's time to party! I'd stop off and pick up a twelve-pack of my favorite beer and that would be the beginning of yet another lost weekend. It was my reward for having trudged through all those days. My own personal pat on the back that I couldn't seem to reach any other way.

There were many people coming and going in my life then, but my constant companion—the one thing I could count on—was getting high. Drugs and alco-hol were the things that kept me going and the yummy twins that awaited me for a threesome at the end of every long week. It's been a long time since my life was anything at all like that, but I still have thoughts of, Okay, tomorrow is Friday and I made it through another week. Where's my reward?

It's not a twelve-pack, an ounce of weed, or a vial of pills ... so what is it now? Candy? Sex? A trip for coffee? Gimmee, gimmee, get me, get me! Something new, something tasty, something, some thing!

In contemplating this, what I realize is that this is still alcoholic thinking holding me hostage. I'm looking outside of myself yet again for something to fill that void. The road has gotten narrow lately in a way I can't describe. I've come to a certain plateau, and there's resistance to continuing the journey. It's not even that it's such a struggle, it's that I feel like I'm looking at this bleak, blank vista ahead of me and I have no desire to take another step.

There are things that new (like teaching) and things that are challenging (like being in a relationship), and yet there's a part of me that's always looking for the treat. Give me something quick and easy! Give me something that's going to instantly make me feel good and give me satisfaction. None of this long-term goal stuff will do!

I sometime feel that I live with a constant, churning impatience with myself and with those around me. Tonight, it's right here, right on the surface demanding answers, demanding satisfaction.

When I came home from work tonight I was exhausted, so I decided to take a nap. As I was falling asleep, a very loud car alarm went off down the street and it continued to shriek as I slept. It was an excellent metaphor for the way I feel, the way I continue to feel in times like this.

Lately, I feel as though there's always this shrieking alarm going off inside of me, wanting something. I can live with it, I can even sleep through it, but it's always there setting my nerves on edge and making me aware of the inner tension of my own hunger, my own insatiable demand for satisfaction.

I want to scream "Shut up! Shut up!" I want to throw rock through the window of the car making the noise. It still wouldn't stop the shrieking, but it might move some of this energy I can't seem to tame.

So here I am. One more night I go toe-to-toe with this thing, wrestling in a grudge match with a faceless, nameless demon that says, "I want, I want, I want .... "

What I have learned in the past twelve years is that my relationship with God and my spiritual practice is the only answer, even when I'm not sure of the question. I am finally in the relationship with the higher self I had been seeking through drugs and alcohol all along. My relationship with God, with myself, is all there is. All there will ever be.

Am I strong enough? Am I willing to commit my life and my heart at an even deeper level to doing whatever it takes to keep moving forward? Am I willing to walk off this damn plateau?

As I write this, I have no cutesy conclusion. All I have is the willingness to accept myself as I am in this moment. I also have the spiritual conviction of knowing the next step I take, whatever it will be, will be sober, and I know I am not alone in this courageous walk.

Thank you, all of you, seen and unseen members of AA, for continuing to take this walk into the unknown with me. You are the treat I truly savor.

Christine P.
North Hollywood, California

Meditation

September 1994

Now that I have survived getting sober and have begun my spiritual journey in recovery, meditation has become a valuable tool in my daily life. Why meditate? Because it helps us to live in the now and is suggested in the Eleventh Step: "Sought through prayer and meditation to improve our conscious contact with God as we understood Him ..."

When I first got sober I was filled with fear and self-loathing. It was suggested that I try to meditate to help with the severe anxiety and insomnia I suffered from. My response to the suggestion was, "But I can't meditate." Yet, I had never tried to meditate; it was hard for me to imagine just sitting still and being with myself.

I have since learned that anyone can meditate. You don't have to be a yogi mystic or join an ashram to learn how. After medicating and anesthetizing myself with alcohol, I found I needed something to be gentle with my vulnerable self. That something for me was meditation.

My life was so full in recovery, I was finding it hard to accomplish all the things that I wanted to do in a day, trying to make up for twenty years of time lost because of active alcoholism. I wanted to get well yesterday, yet I resisted trying meditation because it was new and different. "I can't find the time to meditate, what with meetings, school, and just life in general." My sponsor responded with, "Make the time for yourself! Like meetings, eating well, and exercising, meditation is a wonderful daily gift of self-love. Find a special place, your own private retreat, to meditate for just twenty minutes a day."

I found myself on an emotional roller coaster, as so many of us talk about in the program. I had a hard time concentrating and communicating how I was feeling, other than lousy. I joined a meditation group that met once a week and

I felt frustrated when I first attempted to meditate and nothing happened, other than feeling uncomfortable in my own skin. All my racing thoughts and every little noise around me were irritating distractions. I had a hard time focusing and paying attention. When asked how it was going, I responded, "It's not working for me; there are too many distractions." I was gently told it's normal to have thoughts and noises distract me from clearing my mind, but to just notice them instead of resisting or struggling, gently bringing myself back to my breathing.

I assumed I was doing something wrong. After all, my low self-esteem had me convinced that I could do nothing right. "But how do I meditate? With so much turmoil and stress already in my life, how do I sit quietly and calmly meditate for twenty minutes?" It was suggested that I dress comfortably, sit either cross legged or in a chair, whichever was more comfortable as long as my back was straight, close my eyes, and begin to focus on my natural breathing. I finally stopped resisting and did it, "keeping it simple."

Upon awakening after my daily prayers, I now meditate for twenty minutes in my own private retreat before facing the world.

Meditation has become a daily gift of self-love, just as my sponsor promised it would be. I'm beginning to clear up and have had genuine moments of serenity. Meditation, as part of the Steps, continues to be a valuable tool in helping me improve my conscious contact with my Higher Power. Like anything, meditation gets easier with practice. It has helped me to become less anxious; instead of reacting to every little problem, I'm able to stand back and look for solutions. I still have my moments like every human being, and I'm far from perfect, but I feel better about myself today. In my fourth year of recovery, thanks to Alcoholics Anonymous and the Twelve Steps, I am becoming the woman I was meant to be, "one day at a time."

Nancy D.
Falmouth, Massachusetts

Where It's At

March 2008

During the Christmas holidays in 1966, guess what? I was drunk. My brother, who had recently gotten sober in AA, came to visit me.

"You should go to AA. That's where it's at," he said.

I raved, "I know where it's at! I'm a jazz musician! 'It' is wine, women, and song; drugs, sex, and rock 'n' roll; it's being hip, slick, and cool; it's recognition, fame, and applause. That's where 'it's' at!" I bellowed back.

"Go to AA," my brother calmly repeated. "That's where it's at."

"Okay, smart mouth, what is your idea of 'it'?"

He said, "'It' is anonymous. It has no name, it's the complement to profession-alism. It is 'God as we understood him.' So you can't argue with us. We surrender."

I was astonished. That's all he said. His silence was more convincing than any words. Curious, I went to my first AA meeting on January 2, 1967, and have been sober ever since, by the grace of God and the help of AA.

Dave C.
Richmond, California

With a Little Help from My Friends

November 2001

I came to my first AA meeting after having spent thirty days not drinking, to prove that I wasn't an alcoholic. Following this month of abstinence, I walked into a liquor store and went home with my bottles, saying all the while, "I don't want to do this, I don't want to do this." By evening I was totally drunk, had a huge fight with my husband (during which I threw my glasses at him and broke them), and then—"just to show him"—I called the AA hotline. The one thing I remember from that conversation was being told that the next meeting was a woman's meeting the following evening, at the one church in the area I knew, literally one mile down the street from where we lived.

So I came into the Fellowship, taking Step One whole-heartedly; I knew I was an alcoholic and that my life was unmanageable. But that was as far as I was able to go at the time. I wanted nothing to do with the concept of God, so my sponsor told me that I could use the group as my Higher Power. Since I wanted what those people had, I was willing to do that. So the Sisters in Sobriety became not only my home group, but also my Higher Power.

That was the end of March; in June I had promised to go to Maine to deliver a paper. My husband and I had planned a swing through the northern states to visit friends and family, staying in Maine with a friend with whom I always spent a night drinking whenever we got together. I was anxious about the trip. Looking back, I realize that although I was to some extent on a pink cloud, I was also fear-ful of many things, since sobriety was so new. So one thing I did right was to let my friend know that I was not drinking and I was in AA.

When we got to Maine, it turned out that my friend had planned a party while we were there. When I expressed some fear about that, she reassured me that she wouldn't be drinking and there would be other people who wouldn't be drinking. I was still anxious, since the only way I knew to meet and talk to strangers was to have a few drinks first.

When the evening came, everyone drank. Some left fairly early, but those who stayed to party and to dance were drinking a lot. All except me. You know how I felt. Then the moment came when everyone was in the living room dancing or in clusters "discussing" various topics, and I was sitting alone at the kitchen table (the kitchen was the designated smoking area) smoking cigarettes and feeling left out. And to my immediate left sat a nearly full fifth of Jamesons.

Now Scotch is my drug of choice, but Irish will do in a pinch. I swear, it was speaking to me, calling my name. So I did what I had heard in AA to do—I called on my Higher Power. I conjured up the women's group at the table around me: Susan, Dee, Joanne, Carole, Patsy, the whole crew. And I told them I didn't want to drink but I wanted a drink. That I wanted sobriety but I was sorely tempted. I told them I didn't know what to do.

And they said, "What do you want to do?" And I said, "I don't want to drink." And they said, "So, what do you want to do instead?" and I said, "I want to go to bed." And they said, "So?" and I realized that was what I should do. I hesitated briefly—what would people think if I went to bed in the middle of a party? But I knew that I needed to do what was right for me.

Luckily, the apartment was laid out so that the bedroom we were using was not one anyone needed to go through. I just slipped away to the bedroom, lay awake all of about five minutes, and fell asleep.

The next morning I woke at dawn with a winged heart. I had made it through a difficult situation where there was liquor readily available and did not drink. What joy! I made coffee, went for a walk, came home, and, I must confess, took great pleasure in being obnoxiously cheerful around some seriously hung-over people.

Since then I have found a Higher Power to whom I can pray morning, noon, and night, and whenever I need help. My home group is still Sisters in Sobriety, and though some of the women have moved or moved on, there are always new and wonderful people to welcome to this life-saving Fellowship.

And what I keep discovering over and over again is that this program really works, that it is filled with "firsts," each of which reinforces my faith and gratitude, and that with each one I am witnessing a miracle.

Mary C.
Orangeburg, South Carolina

Life, Not Regrets

July 2007, from PO Box 1980

Today I celebrate eighteen months without a drink.

I'm also divorced two years from a thirty-plus year marriage. One day, after sitting alone, soaked in tears and feeling empty, worthless, and crippled in the smallest task, I reached out and gave my phone number to someone else—they were hurting, too. In that simplest of acts, my world changed.

I thank AA for helping me live my life instead of my regrets.

Valerie
Salt Lake City, Utah

How My Father Twelfth-Stepped Me

July 2004

I was in a county jail, in the darkest moments of my life. I had just been arrested for some very serious charges, which I was guilty of. I was without hope and believed I was never going to get out. My alcoholism (and obsession with drugs) had led me to commit crimes I didn't think I was capable of.

It was then that my dad began to twelfth-step me. I don't think either one of us knew that's what was happening. He was just a father trying to help his lost son, and I was in no position to turn down help from anyone.

He told me he loved me and was going to do everything he could for me. He told me he was angry and hurt by the things I had done, but that he was still going to be there. I didn't know at the time that it was possible to feel anger toward someone yet still treat him with love. The AA program had to teach me that, as it probably had taught my dad. My father has been an active, sober member of AA for over thirteen years now.

I was subsequently sentenced to fifteen years in prison and transferred to a penitentiary. I still believed that my life was over and spent my time involving myself in anything that would distract me from the hopelessness, emptiness, and shame that was always present. Gambling, alcohol, and drugs occupied a lot of my time.

My father was there every step of the way, visiting regularly, accepting countless collect calls, supporting me financially, and just being a dad. He suggested meetings, but I was full of excuses and he didn't push. He just kept loving me.

After more than two years of this, I experienced a series of events which triggered my spiritual awakening. I realized that if I kept doing what I was doing, I was one day going to leave prison the same man who went in—at best. And I knew I would probably repeat the same crimes, if not worse ones. I was terrified by that prospect, enough that I became willing to do something. I started attending AA, and entered a lengthy treatment program available at my institution.

Through God's power (certainly not mine), I was able to shed the destructive behaviors I had been exhibiting. But the emptiness and shame of so many years of drinking and drugging were more present than ever. I was told that the Steps would help, and I was willing to try.

My father was still visiting regularly, but the tone of our visits was definitely changing. Whereas before we had discussed sports or politics, now we started talking about what I was doing in the program. Whatever difficulties I was having, he shared his experience, strength, and hope about similar difficulties. He didn't judge or advise, he just shared. Our visits had become AA meetings, one alcoholic sharing with another.

It was just what I needed. And then one day it hit me like a ton of bricks: My dad was living, breathing evidence that the AA program worked. I didn't need anyone to tell me what it was like, what happened, and what it was like today, because I had personally witnessed, over time, my father's transformation into the honorable man I loved so much.

The joys that have followed have made me feel I'm the most blessed man on earth, though I continue to serve my prison term. In that same visiting room where we spent so many hours, we shed tears as we made amends to each other and put our pasts to rest. In that same room, we got up together and shared our stories with a group of recovering men. And in that same room, we continue to have our two-man meetings to this day.

My father didn't twelfth-step me by sharing his story and then leaving me a book to read. He did it by being a living example, day in and day out for many years, of how AA can make a man more than what he was. And in doing so, he helped me come to believe that I could do the same. That's how it works—one alcoholic sharing with another, even a father and son in the cold, drab visiting room of a prison.

Dave R.
London, Ohio

Sitting in Silence, Listening

November 2009

I n early sobriety it was suggested to me that I think of prayer as talking to God and meditation as listening. That idea took hold. I sobered up in 1972; in 1984 I learned how to meditate at a Catholic retreat center, under a priest who had spent 25 years in Japan studying Zen Buddhism. That was my introduction to the practice of meditation, and it took.

In 1985 I was down and out with chronic fatigue, so I began a meditation meeting in my home, mostly to get me up and out of bed. My group, mostly local women alcoholics, met from 7 to 7:30 A.M., Monday through Friday. There was no talking. It was just sitting in silence, listening, for 30 minutes. At 7:30 I'd gong a gong and we'd all stand in a circle and bow, using the word Namaste, which means "I honor the divine in you." They'd leave and I'd go back to bed.

It's now years later and I'm into my sixth year of healing from chronic fatigue. I believe that there's a touch of good in every single thing. The biggest gift of living with chronic fatigue for 19 years is that I became dedicated to meditation—to listening to God—and I learned how to quiet my mind. The morning meditation ended a few years ago, but a Wednesday night meditation group continues. The best gift of meditation, from my perspective, is that I've been introduced to the Spirit of the Universe by experiencing it in the very breath that I breathe. I love that God is available to all equally, that he's all about love, and that some of us experience that source of love by simply practicing the AA principles in all our affairs.

Linda I.
El Granada, California

It's Showtime

June 2009

Something obviously needed to be done in my 18th month of recovery. I prayed for God to take my will and my life, as he had done early in my sobriety, but my alcoholism was creeping back into my life, demanding to reassert its central place. As my physical and fiscal health returned, I felt my initial elation and freedom slowly turning to a vague dissatisfaction, a mounting sense of "not enough." Enough what? I asked myself, stymied.

My feelings were hurt more frequently, small things began to increasingly irritate me, and the quiet moments I used to relish were becoming (dare I say it?) boring. The spiritual intoxication I had felt while placing my entire faith in taking the Steps was waning. I realized that as the terror of facing myself and my wrongs subsided and as my amends were made and accepted, so had my urgency to leave things in God's hands.

My alcoholism was now counseling me to whip my finances into further shape to make up for lost time, or to finish the book that my drinking had abruptly halted five years ago, or, better yet, to cling to my partner and feed off his 20 years of recovery. I tried to resist by willpower and praying for the strength to thwart my ancient compulsions, petitioning God for balance in my life, but I was clearly failing. Fearful that I would succumb entirely to my old demons, I continued to read the Big Book with my sponsor.

One night while we were reading "The Family Afterward," I felt the solution might lie there. I marked with a star certain lines that jumped out at me. Back home, my partner asked me what I'd gotten out of the reading. I turned to the starred paragraphs and told him, hesitantly, that after months of living in our apartment and rarely going out, I was getting restless. I knew that diving into meaningless activity would only feed my old obsession. I told him I'd like to allow God to replace my spiritual make-believe world with one in which I worked with a great sense of purpose.

I had already commenced work with other alcoholics and much more of God had been revealed, increasing my understanding of him. But the small town we lived in held few work options that appealed to me. My partner had encouraged me to teach reading to the teenagers at the group home where he worked. Others had asked me to work at the community center with young adults and children, and there were other leads.

I had always wanted to work with teens. I thought this might be an avenue.

The next day after my morning meditation, I received a call. The teens at the group home were organizing a talent show, and they asked me to judge. It felt like a sign and, despite the busy holiday season, I accepted with an open mind and a willing heart. I opened the Big Book again and another starred entry made me smile. "We have found nothing incompatible between a powerful spiritual experience and a life of sane and happy usefulness ... So we think cheerfulness and laughter make for usefulness ... We have recovered, and have been given the power to help others."

The teens sang with their hearts and danced with inspiration. Family members in attendance applauded with appreciation at the talent on display. So I thought of something positive to say for each contestant. After the last note, the teens mingled with the audience. We announced the winners, to loud applause. Then I waded forth among the teens and praised the performances of as many as I could. They flushed with success and pride.

And I felt uplifted.

I do not yet know God's design for my work. Nor need I, until he guides me to it. All I need to do is pray that I do my part each day. In this way, each day I turn my ongoing spiritual experience into a sane and happy usefulness among my fellow travelers.

Marie S.
Nome, Alaska

It's a Privilege

December 2003

I woke up on Friday, May 24, and finished off a bottle of vodka. I then went to work and was excused at about 10:30. Although my boss insisted someone else drive, I drove home by myself, stopping for a bottle on the way. My shame and remorse were so great that the only option I was entertaining was suicide. I went to an afternoon haircut appointment and continued to drink afterward. At home, I picked up a gun I had stolen and held it to my head; I couldn't pull the trigger. I shot a round of buckshot into the ceiling instead. I got into my car and drove to a bar ten miles away. Later, someone was kind enough to drive me home. I was in a blackout and came to a few miles from my home. So I decided to return to my automobile, which I promptly crashed into a parked car. I flipped it on impact, and my forearm was crushed. I came to in the hospital to find that my arm had been amputated.

By the grace of a spiritual experience, the help of a chaplain, and the Fellowship, I was able to accept my loss. I have acknowledged my powerlessness and have made the decision to be happy. I am mindful to live unselfishly and quietly, following AA's spiritual principles and the examples of others. I listen and feel for the teaching of my God, and I ask for instruction.

It has been ten months since my loss and I have been given a faith that brings me the courage to be myself, one day at a time. It is only in the moment that I can live, or I would give up. I placed all my marbles on the table, bargaining with alcohol and in denial of life. I have come to understand what a privilege it is to be alive and to have contact with other people, places, and things. I am forever indebted to Alcoholics Anonymous.

Anonymous

I'm Not Broken

December 2009

I am an intellect. I was told early on that this was a simple program and not to complicate it. A couple of years into the program I found myself in a place of turmoil. I was reworking my Steps with a new sponsor and searching daily for aspects of my personality that I wanted to continue to improve. Having worked through the Steps before, I had worked on many of my primary traits already. I was no longer doing a lot of the things that used to leave me ashamed and regretful at the end of the day. I was sleeping contentedly most nights, and I was really starting to enjoy the woman I was seeing in the mirror. There were still things, though, that would plague my daily inventory and were constantly turning around in my mind. The solution suddenly came to me one night while listening to a Big Book study on CD. The speaker was talking about Bill W.'s early experiences prior to the creation of AA. He referred to how Bill had tried self-will, had tried the church, and had even tried working with a psychologist, hoping it would improve his emotional problems enough for him to remain sober. The speaker said, "Thank God that psychology didn't work for Bill and he discovered that the solution lies in a Higher Power. Otherwise, we'd all be sitting around all day psychoanalyzing ourselves instead of turning our problems over to a Higher Power for a solution."

It was like the whole room became still and then something very significant clicked in my mind. I was doing my daily inventory. I knew what character defects were involved, but I had not then turned them over. I was still trying to come up with a solution on my own to fix these defects. In a way, I was still playing God.

And the more I took these problems upon myself to fix, the more I was subconsciously telling myself that I was broken.

A shift took place inside me. I was not broken; I was on the path of recovery. I had a solution today and that solution was my Higher Power. It was such a relief to be reminded that I could surrender my issues to my Higher Power and they would be taken care of. Since that day, I have made a determined effort to focus more on seeing myself as God sees me.

Heather E.
Reston, Virginia

The Path to Power
April 2010

I recently had an experience in AA that I know is not unique, but I wish it upon no one. For a time I was raising my hand to volunteer at my home group; I was active, serving on two different committees and a sub-committee; and I sponsored a handful of guys. If you looked at my life from the outside you would say that I was "doing the deal." I thought I was on top of the world. I was in a happy marriage with a new baby and, despite a downturn of my industry, I was employed. In spite of that, there was an uneasy feeling in my gut, a feeling that I'd been aware of many times before AA and in early sobriety, but that I hadn't felt in close to four years.

I went through the magic equation of Steps Ten and Eleven to search for the cause of the problem, only to find that I was drawing a blank. What was I to do? The thought that I wasn't involved enough in service entered my mind. That's the ticket, I thought. I need another commitment. After all, in early sobriety, any time I got involved more I felt better. When I told my wife that I needed to do more service, she looked at me like I was crazy. She must not understand, I thought.

So there I sat between a rock and a hard place. The Big Book calls it the turning point. I was four years sober and dying of alcoholism in the rooms of AA. Fear began to dominate my life. I couldn't speak of this in AA—or so I thought. After all, I was "Johnny AA." I was not supposed to feel the way I did. My life looked great on the outside. What was I going to do?

Here is where my story takes a turn I never thought could happen. I began to journey back through the Steps. As I went through "The Doctor's Opinion" and the first 57 pages, things began to make sense. When I got to "There Is a Solution" and read how Rowland H. was crushed by the fact that his religious convictions did not spell the necessary spiritual experience, a light turned on for me: My AA convictions did not spell the necessary spiritual experience.

I came across this realization again in "We Agnostics." "If a mere code of morals or better philosophy were sufficient to overcome alcoholism, many of us would have recovered a long time ago." I had been treating AA as that very thing—a better philosophy for life. The result was that I had began to suffer from untreated alcoholism. See, I had thought AA was this magic formula. Go to meetings, get involved, read the book and help others. While all those things are vital to access a spiritual experience, those things are not the spiritual experience. Lack of power is my dilemma. AA is a path to power, not the power.

I took an infinite God and restricted him to an A+B=C formula. In essence, I'd made God finite and I got finite results. What a lonely feeling.

I faced the same proposition at nearly five years of sobriety that I did at six months of sobriety. "God either is or he isn't. What was my choice to be?"

Today here I sit at a new beginning. I am on a new journey with a new God of my understanding. The opportunities, I believe, are truly infinite. I will do my best to not turn AA into something it is not—a religion. I can get wrapped up in the principles and rituals of AA and forget the only thing that truly keeps me sober and sane: God. My life depends on a constant contact with him and an infinitely growing relationship.

Jason E.
Greendale, Wisconsin

SECTION TWO

Where Two or More Are Gathered

In the July 1953 Grapevine, Bill W. reports that when Dr. Bob was preparing his story for the book *Alcoholics Anonymous*, in 1939, he put one paragraph of the story in italics to emphasize its importance. Speaking of his co-founder, Dr. Bob said, "Of far more importance was the fact that he was the first living human with whom I had ever talked, who knew what be was talking about in regard to alcoholism from actual experience."

That is as clear a definition of an AA meeting as anything could be. Our entire history-making, life-saving program is modeled on that one event: two alcoholics sharing their experience, strength, hope ... and their gift of desperation.

Every day, in every corner of the globe, thousands of similar meetings are held. They may involve many more alcoholics; they may be held under trees or in trailers, church basements, in the rectories of cathedrals or even—as in Las Vegas—in the back rooms of bars. But they are our touchstones, our simple hope. They are the keys to the kingdom of sobriety.

The account that begins this section may very well be one of the most poignant we've ever read, taking the word "meeting" to a sacred new level.

Equally moving is the answer to one member's question: "How do deaf meeting-goers connect at the end of a meeting, when they need their hands to sign the prayer?" "Will you go to any lengths?" demanded the message in all caps on a desperate drinker's computer screen, just in the nick of time. Here's how it feels to stand in your driveway with tears streaming down your cheeks after a hospital stay as cars full of sober people arrive to bring you a surprise meeting. And then we read, "I could not believe that any human being would pick up a stranger and head for a church in a part of the county where neither of them had ever been before. But it happened."

Here is an impromptu meeting at Ground Zero, and an account of one chairman's "perfect" meeting, ruined, he thought, by an old homeless bum whose message of dignity was powerful enough to change at least one nervous meeting chairman's life.

"Yes." Dr. Bob might be nodding right about now. "That's exactly what I meant."

One-Room Schoolhouse

June 2005

I was at the local electronics shop when a guy I barely recognized came up to me. "You said something once that I'll never forget," he said. At first, I had no idea what he was talking about. Then he reminded me about the toughest night of my life. I'd been going to AA meetings for a dozen years when my oldest son came down with what the doctors thought was the West Nile virus, a form of encephalitis. He was having seizures that the hospital couldn't stop. My son, for reasons of his own, had followed me into AA. He was a wonderful kid and he had turned his life around. He'd been a stage manager for a big local theater operation. But he left that, went back to school, got an MBA, joined a bank, and was a rising star in their financial operations. He'd just gotten married. Everything was terrific until he got sick, suddenly and frighteningly. Everybody rallied around.

My role was to sit with him overnight, holding his hand and praying. He was on a respirator, but I had the idea to hold a meeting. After all, there were two of us, both in AA. So I began. I talked for fifteen minutes, then I said to my less-than-conscious son, "So, why don't we start the comments with you?" I like to think he heard me though he didn't say anything or even move a muscle. Yet, somehow, the idea that we were both together, sharing something that had helped us through life's worst moments kept me going. My son died the next day. I thought, for a while, that I would die too. But I didn't, and I didn't drink. Friends in AA helped and eventually I told the story of the midnight meetings at the hospital. Then, at that store, somebody came up and told me how much my experience had helped him face a tough time of his own. That's what I like about AA meetings. They are like little one-room schoolhouses. Each of us shares. And each of us learns.

Jon A.
Chicago, Illinois

EXCERPTED FROM

Faith Among the Ruins

September 2002

I was at Ground Zero. I bowed my head. It was just that simple. The grief was so profound I don't think I ever imagined being strong enough to contain it. But I did. A young police officer came up and stood beside me. The large yellow crane was just yards from us. Puffs of smoke collected like clouds on a mountaintop over the big hills of coiled steel. It didn't look so different from the way it looked on TV. My imagination had done me a good enough service, had prepared me properly. And my program had prepared me for the rest. I had the face on me of all the men and women who have helped me throughout the years, all the stories shared, the pain and the joy, the grisly and the miraculous.

Just the week before, I had sat in a meeting where the topic of "doubting I'm an alcoholic" played out. Later I thought that none of us had gotten it right. It isn't whether you were the worst drunk, or "not really" a drunk, or how much you drank. It was about the obsession with drink. In the end, I hardly needed to swallow a thimbleful to go into a blackout; it was the minute-to-minute obsession with that thimbleful that finally stopped me cold. There simply wasn't any room to think about food, or exercise, or sleeping properly, let alone true feelings. I don't think I ever thought of my heart, either as a muscle or a vehicle for spiritual strength.

After fifteen minutes, I went back to work, after having my boots (a good choice) sprayed by my friends in yellow. As the hours moved along, I felt ridiculously strong for a fifty-year-old vet of the rooms. I carried a lot of water back and forth, washed and dried pans and utensils, worked the ovens (some heated by Sternos), unpacked and layered food in pans, carted boxes of beverages, served up the brownies hot, and resisted the strudel.

Around nine o'clock, I took a plate and served myself, then headed for a seat at one of the tables. After the dinner rush, the place was not too crowded. I spotted a young, sandy-haired construction worker seated alone, his battered hard hat next to his plate. "You feel like company, or you want to eat alone?" I asked. He pushed his hat to the side and nodded for me to sit down opposite him. I never got his name.

"Where do you live?" he asked.

"Tenth and University," I said.

"Oh, that's near Round the Clock," he said.

I'd had sponsors who worked there. It was an all-night bar and restaurant. "That's a party place, isn't it?" I asked, forking rice and vegetables into my mouth.

"Actually, I stopped drinking there," the young man said, eyeing me. I wondered how he thought I might respond. I felt a slight smile coming to my face, but I didn't want to move in on his territory so fast.

"Good for you," I said, munching a piece of soft summer squash.

"That was twelve years ago. Now I have a wife and two kids. My kids have never seen me drunk."

"That's great. Really great." I smiled.

"Yeah," he said, glancing sidelong at a few of his colleagues. I had wondered why he was sitting by himself. "Sometimes it's not so easy. It's difficult to take my family to my co-worker's parties. I realize their kids see things my kids don't. My kids ask me a lot of questions."

I had stopped eating, and we were looking at each other as if we'd known each other for a while. "I've been in AA for twenty years," I said. It hardly seemed like news.

He told me how hard it had been to stay sober. He'd been in and out a number of times before he put down his last drink. He didn't go to as many meetings as he used to. I told him that I always feel like I've taken care of myself after a meeting, whatever it's been like.

"Can I tell you something, Connie?" he said. I had forgotten that my name was written on duct tape across my shoulder. I sat still, feeling glad that I'd come all the way across time to be there for him. "I've been frightened. I mean really frightened. When I go up on those mounds of twisted wire, my legs shake, and I feel like my heart's going to burst in my ears. I have two little boys and a wife and a home. None of us workers have any idea what we're standing on out there. Something shifts and my boys have no father."

Bill and Dr. Bob were suddenly there with us. One alcoholic helping another stay sober. One day at a time. This is the way it works, planned or seemingly at random, it all comes round and back to that. None of us is alone.

We talked a little while longer. Then he stood up, at the same time trying to take his hard hat and his tray.

"I'll get the tray," I said, a little too sharply. He was about my son's age. He hesitated.

Pulling his tray closer to me, I said, "No. I'll do my job and you do yours." I didn't watch him go.

Connie C.
New York, New York

The Perfect Meeting

September 2005

At only eight months sober, I had been elected secretary of my home group, a most important and noteworthy position. It's important, for it is really the secretary's meeting—he or she does all the work to keep it going and interesting. To top things off, I had, all on my own mind you, managed to obtain a most popular speaker. I had already chosen a super topic, and was sure they were all going to say, "Thanks, Gregoire. Thanks to you this is a truly great meeting."

"My" meeting started off fine, on time, like it should, in the church basement. I sure was proud of myself.

The meeting approached half-time. Most of the people who commented on the speaker's fine talk, the "format," knew me. I recognized them and allowed them to speak, knowing they would have good comments to make.

Even the topic I had "suggested" was met with great approval—it was most unusual, no one had ever thought of it; why, it wasn't even in the Big Book, nor thought up by Bill W. or any of the old-timers. All right, here it is: What would you lose if, after your time so far in AA, you decided to pick up just one drink? Yes, it was unusual, even startling, I might add, and it just "came to me." Would you call that "inspired"? Wow!

Then came the tragedy.

I would never have anticipated it. Some bum had been let into my meeting. Well, he was sober I guess, but look at him!—in rags, a disgrace. How awful. And they let him in! To "my" meeting.

Oh, horror of horrors, he had his hand up. What nerve! He wanted to speak at my meeting. Well, not to worry, he will be ignored, I thought. Still, his hand was up, and after everyone had said good, appropriate things in response to my unusual question. Oh well, let him speak. What can he possibly say that might spoil my meeting?

The old bum cleared his throat and started to speak: "You ask what I would lose, if after all I have learned in AA this past year, I now would pick up just one drink?"

"Well," he said, "I would lose, most of all, my dignity as a man." There was silence. I don't even remember the meeting ending, the clearing up, people getting their coats and leaving.

I sat silent in my secretary chair. Did I imagine the chair had shrunken in size? The old man was the last to leave, and suddenly I heard my voice calling to him: "Thank you, brother." I was shaking now, but blurted out: "Thank you for what you said." Silently, slowly, I put on my coat and held the door open for this old man who had . . . dignity—a concept I hadn't understood until then and didn't realize I would find at this "perfect" meeting.

Gregoire G.
San Francisco, California

On My Knees into the World Wide Web of Recovery

October 2002

I had been drinking at home without respite for years. I had tried many times to convince myself that this was the last bottle of gin I would buy. My intentions were always good, but the two-liter bottle was gone in one day. As I was pouring one of the last drinks from the bottle, such anxiety invaded me that I had to go to any length to buy another one. At times, I would look under pillows, couches, and beds, and in drawers, boxes, and my children's piggy banks, in a desperate search for coins to complete the $14.00 I needed to buy that bottle. Driving while intoxicated was not even a concern. My focus was only on the sign that said LIQUOR STORE. My heaven, my rest, my solution—so I thought.

My drinking had progressed to the point that the only time I wasn't consuming alcohol was during my four restless hours of sleep at night. I slowly came to realize that alcohol was not doing for me what it used to do. The laughter I used to enjoy had turned to tears. I avoided social events like the plague. The jokes were not funny any more. The long and often-forgotten phone conversations had become silence. My heaven had become hell. Only one possibility lay ahead, and that was death. I had lost all interests, had isolated from everybody, had hidden from loved ones, and was ready to die, without even leaving a note behind, or saying good-bye to my children. In an attempt to soothe my inner turmoil and pain, I cut my arms to distract myself from my agonizing soul. Alcohol gave me the courage to do such a thing to myself. But at least the burning pain in my arms was visible, explainable, and of course, affordable.

One day, invaded by physical symptoms of alcoholism, I sat at my desk with my bottle nearby, and turned on my computer. I searched for a recovery chat room and entered the first site that I found. My hands were so shaky that I had difficulty typing. My vision was blurred, and I was rocking slightly from side to side. I had not showered in days and had hardly eaten. I started reading what was being written in the chat room, and finally dared to hit the keys and type "Hello." The greetings and cheerfulness on the screen made me feel safe and in awe of the fact that actual people were having a conversation with me via the Internet. They were typing right there, for me, drunk, desperate, sitting in my little office, at my little desk, the screen in front of my blood-shot eyes and my shrinking soul.

They asked me if I was in recovery, and I answered that I wanted to be, but that I had a bottle of gin by my side and had been drinking nonstop for years. When I had to answer the question "What fears are making you drink?" I could not find any answer, except: "Fears? I have no fears. I am fine." When I had to answer the question "Why are you drinking today?" I could only reply, "Because I have to." When someone typed in upper case, "TO WHAT LENGTH ARE YOU WILLING TO GO TO GET WHAT WE HAVE?" I started to cry. When I read on the screen, there in my little room, "God does not want you to hurt yourself," I started to shake. I was told that I had to make a choice, a decision, an admission, but I was not quite ready yet. When I was told to empty my bottle of gin in the sink, I asked if they wanted to kill me, because I could not imagine living without a drink.

I was in that chat room for hours with folks I had never seen, folks whose real names I did not know and whose home state, country, or background I couldn't guess. But none of those details mattered. I knew they could help me; I felt that I was in the right place. The next day, January 21, 2001, I looked at my bottle with shaking hands, took the last drink at nine o'clock in the morning, and logged on to the chat room again. After a couple of hours the symptom started again: the dry heaves, the shivers, the panic. So, I typed in that little screen, from my little room, with my tiny courage, that I had finished my bottle and was not feeling too well.

After a couple hours of sleep, when the withdrawal symptoms were still very strong, I hurt my back, and the only position I could type from was on my knees. The God of my understanding sure has a way of letting me know what the next step is. I typed for days and evenings while on my knees, with tears rolling down my face, my hands shaking uncontrollably, and the pain in my body and soul as strong as knives being pulled in and out. On my knees into the World Wide Web of Recovery! Several people took the responsibility of coming back into the chat room and talking to me during those days. One at a time, they helped me out. I waited with terror for a possible seizure.

I was told to eat chocolate for the withdrawal, to take a shower to warm up, to pray, to drink water. You see, I could not even think about those things myself. I was a lost soul. They took me by the hand and guided me into a new day and into what I now know is a new life and a true gift, the present.

Seven days after I stopped drinking, I walked myself into a rehab as a part-time outpatient for six weeks. But I did not know how to behave in my own house without drinking. I needed constant support from sober people, so I kept on logging on to the recovery chat room. I finally started to feel less isolated, less lost, less dying. I felt that there was a solution and that I finally might have a choice.

The following weekend, I attended my first AA meeting. I will never forget the folks in that room. I still hear in my mind and soul the speaker that evening. I will never forget the sense of belonging and the love and tolerance I felt. I will never forget coming home. At my second meeting, I found a sponsor, who told me, as we stood up to close the meeting and said the Lord's Prayer while holding hands: "This is where you hang on for dear life." And I understood the First Step: I was powerless over alcohol and my life had become unmanageable.

It is indeed a "we" program. I cannot do it alone. But with folks in recovery around the world, on the world wide web, in church basements, in hallways, in parks, with blessed servants who convey the language of the heart, and with my Higher Power, I know today that I do have a chance to live a reasonably happy life, as long as I keep on trudging on this road that the Twelve Steps of AA help me build. And to this day, I have not found it necessary to pick up a drink.

Today, I am a trusted servant for an online recovery site and the secretary of my home group, and I volunteer to help women in recovery coming out of situations involving abuse and violence. My children trust me again, my family is learning to respect and discover me, and my soul rejoices. I have found rewards beyond all my expectations, and I know that it will get better. Every day will bring me challenges, but now I have the spiritual tools to cope with life on life's terms. I am no longer the prisoner of my past, my wants, my sorrows, my addictions.

In the last year, I have had the privilege of meeting several people from the recovery chat room. I drove many miles to have lunch with some of them, and welcomed others to my home. Never did I think for one minute that through my computer screen I would find soulmates who would actually share my food, life, pains, and laughter while we looked into one another's eyes. My little room is now as vast as I let it be, and my computer is filled with recovery.

Anonymous

Inside an ASL Meeting

October 2004

I attend AA meetings daily in Hawaii. Recently, my three favorite groups debated the same controversy. Should we pay to hire an American Sign Language (ASL) interpreter? It wasn't certain there were deaf or hard of hearing alcoholics that wanted AA in our area, but some members thought if the service was provided, deaf people with a drinking problem would "hear" of the program and perhaps attend.

I have a deaf brother, and deafness is a very emotional issue for me, so I stayed out of the debate. I knew if I opened my mouth, my alcoholic evil twin (part politician, part game show host) would seize control of the home group meeting for "the good of AA"—according to me. Without my input, one group decided to pay for an ASL interpreter, one group voted the idea down, and one is still developing their plan.

Thinking about the controversy reminded me of one of the most powerful experiences of my sobriety. In July 2001, I was attending an ASL summer camp in Vancouver, Washington. We studied and slept at the campus of the Washington State School for the Deaf.

On my first day there, I called the AA central office in Vancouver, told them where I was staying, and asked for a nearby meeting.

When I arrived at the club, I discovered it was a meeting for the deaf, conducted only in sign language. There were about twenty deaf people in the room. I am far from fluent in ASL, but I do have some basic signing skills. I considered leaving, but then I thought, "You need an AA meeting and somehow you found this one—so why not sit and see what happens?"

After only a few minutes I knew one thing for sure. There are AA emotions and attitudes that transcend language, and these twenty deaf people had a warm, strong, vibrant home group.

I could understand perhaps half of what was shared. However, I usually got the gist. When deaf members shared their reasons for drinking, they used the same excuses I had used. When they signed of freedom from alcohol and the joy of AA recovery, their hands and faces expressed peace, relief, and optimism as eloquently as any speaker I'd ever heard.

During the break, one of the members "told" me that this deaf AA group paid for a voice interpreter once a week so that hearing alcoholics could benefit from the meeting. I was still pondering that one thirty minutes later when the meeting neared closing. As we rose to form a circle, I thought, "How can we sign the Serenity Prayer while holding hands?"

Pondering this, I thought it was too bad they couldn't enjoy the physical connection during the prayer that we do in hearing meetings. Then one member signed to me and I noticed everyone's feet were touching. I gently pushed my shoes against the shoes of my neighbor's and signed the prayer. Power poured from my feet and hands to my heart.

John W.
Kihei, Hawaii

Summer of Discontent

February 1978

It was the summer of my discontent. I turned forty-one and marched reluctantly into middle age. I also celebrated my twelfth AA birthday and stumbled into an emotional puberty in my spiritual growth.

Believe me, approaching the menopausal years and experiencing mental adolescence simultaneously is no picnic. I was grumpy, grouchy, and crabby. Previous AA depressions had usually been short—a few hours, or maybe a day or two at most. But this time was different. My discontent dragged on for weeks.

I didn't want to drink, but I seethed with unspoken resentments. I was restless. I wanted to run away from home and join a circus. I craved fun and excitement. I longed for a meaningful career, but was willing to work only part-time. In short, I was nuts.

I continued to attend AA meetings, but as the Big Book states, "... obviously you cannot transmit something you haven't got." My head wasn't on straight, so I had nothing to give. Pride prevented me from asking for help. I kept hurting. Plenty.

"My name is Joyce, and I'm an alcoholic. I'm really down tonight. I've been depressed for weeks. I'll pass and listen." There! The words were out. Pain had overcome pride, and I had let my group know I felt rotten. Right away, I felt a little less rotten.

No one commented on what I said, but after the meeting, George came over and put his hands on my shoulders. "You need to talk to someone," he said. "Let's have lunch tomorrow." I agreed.

At lunch, I blurted out all my frustrations, half-baked longings, and resentments to George. Not long before, he had lived soberly through his own crisis of middle-age depression, and he listened calmly. George had just short of a year's sobriety. His head was on straight, and he had something to give.

"Why don't you practice the Serenity Prayer?" he asked. "Accept being forty-one. Enjoy it. Have fun. Remember—no one is stopping you from doing anything you want to do, except you yourself."

He was right, of course. But since I didn't know what I wanted, how could I change anything? I felt less mixed-up after sharing with George, and I gained some insight. I had been slipshod with my program.

I reaffirmed that I was powerless and that my life was unmanageable. I came again to believe that God could restore me to sane thinking. That restoration opened my eyes to a harsh truth: Some time during my middle-age puberty, my working of Step Three had become perfunctory. I had been rattling off, "PleasehelpmetostaysoberThywillnotminebedoneGodblesseveryoneAmen."

Then I would charge into the day, resentments churning, and glower at my husband, my co-workers, and anyone else who crossed my path. Such hostility! No wonder I had been depressed. I needed to take an inventory, and Step Ten wouldn't be enough this time. I'd been skating on some very thin ice. I got out pen and paper and started my fifth Fourth Step.

For openers I wrote, "I'm grumpy, grouchy, and crabby!" I listed my resentments as Chapter 5 suggests. While I checked other faults, I learned I was self-centered and full of false pride.

On the asset side, I wrote that I was sober, that I was determined, with the help of God and AA, to be a better person, that I didn't have a defeatist attitude, and that I was teachable and willing.

When I analyzed my resentments, one word kept leaping out at me: ungrateful. I was taking everything for granted, including sobriety. I had no problems that were not the product of my own discontent. The ice was thinner than I had realized.

I wasted no time before working Step Five. I shared my inventory with my sober alcoholic husband. He had lived almost unscathed through my growing pains by adeptly turning me over daily to his Higher Power.

My depression lifted after I had completed Steps Four and Five. I was back on the AA path, and I applied the remaining Steps.

I learned I had to practice gratitude in my daily life, just as I practiced the Twelve Steps. Saying, "Thank You, God" wasn't enough. I had to feel gratitude in my heart to be happy. A man at a speaker meeting put it perfectly. "I have to keep gratitude alive," he said.

Alive!, I thought. That was the key. Each day was full of blessings waiting to be counted. I started writing daily lists of blessings. Sobriety, faith in God, the AA program, my husband, good health, and AA friends headed each list. However, no joy was too small to be counted—from a tasty breakfast to a purring cat to a friend's warm smile.

From another speaker, I heard, "Happiness isn't getting what you want. Happiness is enjoying what you have."

My summer of discontent vanished into an autumn of renewed growth and love for AA. I cannot afford to take sobriety for granted, and I cannot allow my working of the Steps to become rote recitations. I need and love meetings.

I'm almost forty-two now, and I've never felt better. My husband tells me I've never looked better. I'm barely a teenager in AA years, and therefore subject to fits of adolescent restlessness. But now I know how to defeat discontent. I've learned what to do to keep my gratitude alive. I count my blessings and enjoy them all, large and small.

J. B.
Green Valley, Arizona

The Receiving End

June 2007

I was introduced to AA seven years ago, when the judge ordered temporary custody of my daughters to their father. I attended AA meetings for one reason only and that was to get my daughters back. Once this happened, AA would be history. I recall feeling pity for all those people who did not have the willpower to stop drinking on their own. I went to speaker meetings mostly, but could not relate. I was comparing their stories to mine, never identifying. I really didn't think I needed AA in my life to stop drinking.

I had never considered myself shy until I went to AA. I was withdrawn and didn't want anyone to know me, nor did I want to know them. I wasn't interested in their friendship, as I wasn't planning on being there long anyway. I wasn't impressed with the Fellowship; actually I thought they were a bit on the cold side. I was sure that if I stopped drinking it would mean staying home every night knitting or doing some other boring activity. That was not my idea of a happy life.

After several attempts at getting sober, bouncing in and out of AA, my drinking was progressing rapidly and I still didn't have my daughters back. My life was spiraling out of control. I was sick and tired of being sick and tired. Guilt, remorse, and shame were my daily companions. For the first time in my life, death scared me. I knew my drinking had to stop. With each passing day, I became worse.

One afternoon after drinking, the voices I had heard in AA began to haunt me. I kept hearing these same words repeatedly in my head. "You don't have to do this alone" and "You never have to feel like this again." It was time! I made a phone call to Johnny, a childhood friend of forty years who I knew was in AA. We talked for a few minutes and he invited me to his house for a meeting. In desperation, I did just that. Johnny made it a point of calling me daily and when he couldn't reach me he would leave messages such as: "It is a great day to be sober. Keep coming. And, Cindy, I love you." A few weeks had passed when I realized I was staying sober and was looking forward to Johnny's phone calls. This was amazing. I started attending AA meetings every day, joined a group, and became the chip person. I began talking to other alcoholics, took phone numbers, and gave them mine. I had met some nice people in the Fellowship and was becoming a bit social. I was actually enjoying AA.

A few months later, my doctor told me I would need an operation that would lay me up for about eight weeks. The day after my surgery, Johnny came to see me in the hospital. He sat on my bed and I looked up at him and asked what I was going to do about meetings. I was worried how I was going to stay sober without AA. Johnny told me not to worry, picked up his cell phone, and called another alcoholic named Ray. His exact words were, "We need to get a meeting at Cindy's this Saturday, okay?" and he hung up. I smiled thinking how sweet that was of him but did not really expect it to happen. After all, I knew very few people in AA. Why would they care if I stayed sober?

That Saturday morning, my girlfriend Patty, whom I had met in AA also, showed up with pastries as Johnny informed us that a few people were going to be coming to my house. They made coffee and Johnny set up chairs in the living room. I thought maybe three or four people from AA would show up. They started coming in and I was in shock every time I saw another face. I couldn't believe this. I heard motorcycles coming up the street and assumed there must be a bike rally going on in town. My mouth dropped and my body was trembling as I watched the bikes pull into my driveway. I was yelling "Oh my God!" with tears of joy streaming down my face.

I had read in AA literature how they used to do this years ago, and now it was happening to me. I was filled with gratitude and happiness. I will always remember that day as the turning point in my recovery. A spiritual awakening. What an incredible feeling it was.

Those meetings continued three times a week for the next seven weeks. I am now back on my feet and able to attend other meetings again. We decided to keep the Saturday meeting going at my house.

I am proud to say that I have a sponsor, attend a Twelve-Step study, and go to meetings daily. I do what others have shown me in order to stay sober. I start my day on my knees, read the AA literature, and at night, I end on my knees again, thanking my Higher Power for another day of sobriety.

My daughters are in my custody now, and for that, I feel truly blessed. I am enjoying the sober life I am living today, all of which began by one alcoholic reaching out and helping another, and so the story goes. My message is to keep coming, don't try to do this on your own, and please, get phone numbers and use them—let somebody get to know you. And, oh, by the way, did I mention I didn't have to take up knitting?

Cindy B.
Haverhill, Massachusetts

Powerless Equals Free

September 1984

D uring the quiet time of my regular Friday night meeting, I prayed, "Dear God, I need a miracle to keep from drinking tonight."

When it was my turn to comment, I could only say what I was thinking. I announced that this was my last AA meeting. I was tired of fighting the desire to drink. I was miserable, and I was giving up.

If anyone addressed a comment to me, I didn't hear it. I sat through the rest of the meeting feeling sorry for myself because I had tried for four months, and now I would fail, just as I had always known I would.

When the meeting was over, I scurried to the literature table and pretended to be absorbed in reading. The woman who had brought me to the meeting found me and told me that she would like to go to the restaurant where the group usually gathered after the meeting. Since she was driving, I guessed I had no choice. I considered asking her to drop me off at a bar, but I decided that if I had waited four months to drink, I could wait until she wouldn't be involved.

I tried to become invisible as I walked into the section of the restaurant that we AAs took over on Friday nights. A few people tried to talk to me, and some even teased me about the lemon-sucking look on my face. I attempted some wan smiles and thought that soon they would never have to see me again. Out of the corners of my downcast eyes, I noticed a man pulling up a chair to our table. I remembered seeing him at a different meeting a few weeks earlier. He had said then that he lived in Boston and came to Chicago on business occasionally. Although it didn't seem to bother him that he didn't know anyone, I felt a little sorry for him. I said hello and told him I remembered him from the earlier meeting. Then, he started to speak to someone else, and I went back to staring into my coffee cup.

A little later, it got quiet at our table, and I saw that he and I were the only ones still sitting there. Everyone else had gotten up to circulate among people they knew at other tables. He asked me what was wrong, and I told him.

"What Step are you on?" he asked.

"I'm working on my Fourth Step," I replied, proud of my progress despite my present condition.

"Sounds to me like you never took the First Step." He was smiling, but I knew he was serious.

Who did this man think he was? I had been attending five or six meetings a week ever since my first meeting. I had zipped through the first three Steps and soon would be finished with the Fourth—and this man was telling me I had never taken the First Step! I tried to control my anger as I told him that I certainly wasn't on the First Step, and that Alcoholics Anonymous just wasn't going to work for me, because I was different. Other people seemed real happy to be sober, but I was unhappy.

He remained calm. "If you're thinking drinking, you never took the First Step in your gut. You need to get brutally honest with yourself and admit that you're powerless over alcohol. You may have said it up there" (he pointed to my head), "but you never admitted it down there" (he pointed to my stomach).

I opened my mouth to defend myself. Suddenly, I was seeing a little movie of myself riding home from work on the bus. Every night, the fantasy was the same. I would gaze longingly at each bar we passed and imagine how it would be next time. Next time I drank, I would be nicely dressed, and I would look positively elegant as I lifted the narrow-stemmed glass of white wine to my perfectly lip-sticked lips. And I would always drink only in "nice" bars, not the kind of hole in which I used to chugalug beer.

The audio portion of this advertising-induced idealization was a sort of litany I chanted in my mind: "I have learned my lesson. I have paid my dues. I am able to work now. I am not yellow anymore. I can fit into my clothes today. I can eat breakfast today, and never again will I forget to eat. I will always look good and sip slowly. Never, ever will I again sit alone in my filthy apartment and swill a case of beer. Today, I know how to drink."

I came back to the present with the thought that this was the first time I had seen my daily reverie from outside myself. It looked pretty dumb from that perspective, especially if I took into consideration the fact that I had never in my life known when I would stop drinking once I had started. The cutoff usually came when I passed out. I couldn't point to a single instance in my life where I had controlled my drinking and it hadn't controlled me.

If it had always been the same sad story in the past, how could I possibly think the future would be different? At that moment, I saw the truth: If I had actually admitted—in my gut—that I was powerless over alcohol, I wouldn't be wasting my time fantasizing about the next drink.

The woman who had brought me was waiting to leave. As I slipped on my coat, I was still trying to think of something to say to this man. He waved a finger at me. "If you can't surrender, just accept. Just take that First Step in your gut, and you won't be miserable anymore."

I thanked him and left.

By the time I got home, I was singing out loud. I felt lighter than I could ever remember feeling. I could surrender. I was powerless. And being powerless was great, because I could stop thinking about drinking and start thinking about sobriety—and living.

I had asked God for a miracle, and He gave me one by sending someone to tell me that he had already given me one if I would just accept it.

I never saw that man again, but I have been able to accept my powerlessness over alcohol for six years now, one day at a time. And God has continued to send me many miracles since the first one that occurred the day he gave me courage and willingness to go to my first AA meeting.

M.O.

Oak Park, Illinois

A Power Greater Than Alcohol

May 1984

What a fool I would be to say I cannot believe in a power greater than myself. I had a power so much greater than myself that I long ago lost count of how many days I spent worshiping that bottle of Scotch. But it was certainly a power greater than me. I prayed to God, but I believed it was a drink that would make me feel better. I was so insane that I thought booze would bring me sanity. If it was a rough day—and finally, every day was a rough day—then what I believed I needed was a drink.

There was even ritual to my worship. Scotch was the ultimate expression of my higher power. It deserved to be poured over lots of ice into a very special glass—a large one. I attributed all sorts of marvelous qualities to alcohol-power. It would bring me relaxation, elation, wisdom, sophistication—and would even turn me into a sex kitten. So I believed.

I began my worship by consuming alcohol. But in the end, alcohol consumed me. In return for my worship, it brought me heartburn, diarrhea, shivers, shakes, fog, numbness, slurred speech, stumbling gait, red eyes, bloated body, foul breath, sexual oblivion, guilt, grief, and fear. If I forget that alcohol is an inanimate god, an idol, it is waiting still to reward my worship with insanity and death.

Surely, I could come to believe in a higher power that would reward my adoration a little more decently than that.

I went to my first AA meeting on December 3, 1981. I arrived in the car of a stranger that I had first talked to on the telephone just hours earlier. I could not believe that any human being would pick up a stranger and head for a church in a part of the county where neither of them had ever been before. But it happened.

I could not believe that what I felt at that meeting was real. Yet the twelfth-stepper who brought me said those I heard around that first table were sincere. If that was the case, then I wanted what they had. So I came back to see if I could come to believe in a power greater than myself—or than alcohol.

My sponsor, who offered her sponsorship to me unasked, told me to make not taking a drink the most important thing in my life, to go to as many meetings as I could, to use the telephone any hour of the day or night, and not to let religion get in the way of coming to believe in a Higher Power.

In the book *Came to Believe*, a California AA recalls an old-timer's use of a metaphor in the Big Book: "'A person walking into a dark room does not worry about understanding electricity,' he said. 'He just finds the switch and turns on the light.' He explained that we can turn on the switch of spirituality by simply asking God each morning for another day of sobriety and thanking him at night for another beautiful sober day. He said, 'Do it mechanically if you really don't believe in it. But do it every day. There is probably no one who really understands the wonderful ways of the Higher Power, and we don't need to. He understands us.'"

What a message for me—after all those years of trying to understand God (when I wasn't too busy trying to be God). And I wasn't particularly thankful for sobriety, just for waking up without the morning fog. So I began a new ritual in my life, a program brought to me by AA. My morning prayer began grudgingly, before I even opened my eyes to shut off the alarm. "Thank you, God, that I'm alive and awake without a hangover." At bedtime, it was: "Thank you, God. I'm going to bed without having had a drink today."

As for being restored to sanity—well, some of us are sicker than others, and God isn't finished with me yet. But at least I'm sane enough to be where I need to be right now. And I believe that if I keep coming to AA meetings, then I'll continue to come to believe that a power greater than myself can restore even me to sanity. I see with my own eyes that a Higher Power restores sanity to you—to members of a fellowship that transforms church basements into sanctuaries of shared experience, strength, and hope. Thank you for being here for me. I'm learning to love you.

V.L.
St. Louis, Missouri

Not Alone in the Room

April 2002

A s I rode my bicycle against the wind (I can't drive again until 2003), I wondered who I'd see at the meeting. I sure hoped Bill would be there. He'd been hanging on now for over twenty days, and I was always so happy when he walked into the room. I had the keys with me, but I was hoping that the doors would be unlocked and that someone would already be there. It was the scheduled meeting time, but the room was still empty. My heart sank and I felt immediate resentment and sadness. I contemplated turning around and going home, as I had done in the past, but something called me to the door and down the stairs.

When I unlocked it and went in, slowly at first and then as if I owned the place, an overwhelming feeling of peace and ease came over me. It washed over me the way the feeling of warmth and ease had done so many times before when I took that first drink.

I plopped down on the couch and began to read the daily reflection for the day; then I picked up the Grapevine and read a story. Irritability and discontent were lifted, and love and serenity entered my heart.

Wow! What's going on? I thought. Why am I not feeling resentful that once again the doors are not open for the alcoholic who still suffers? (Don't they know you can be sober and still suffer?) I'd had a bad day and there was no one there to listen to, or to share with, but even so, I was okay.

I contemplated this new thought and I realized that I was not alone in the room. For the first time in my life, I didn't feel alone.

You see, in the past I had fallen prey to loneliness (part of the HALT we watch out for), and as result I had chosen to drink again for one night after almost three years' sobriety. But because I was willing, went to meetings, got a sponsor, read the Big Book, worked the Steps, invited a God of my understanding into my life, prayed, had faith in a Higher Power, and helped others, the desire to drink was lifted. Not only had the miracle of not drinking occurred, but my thinking had changed and, therefore, my actions were different. I suddenly realized that God had done for me what I hadn't been able to do for myself.

I got off the couch and sat down at the head of the table where the chairperson usually sits. With all the empty chairs, and the only sound coming from the slight hum of the fan, I was humbled. God had a plan for me and it was a good one. I had been recently searching for who and what my Higher Power was. I just hadn't felt him working in my life, as I had lost touch with him, and I'd been afraid of drinking again if something didn't happen soon. But I realized that night that God had not left me. I had left him.

With work, kids, AA, and church, I had a very busy life, now. I just hadn't been still enough for my Higher Power to enter my life. I wasn't listening to my Higher Power's answers. Because there was no one in the meeting room that night, I was able to hear the answer: I was not alone after all.

Linda B.
Palmer, Alaska

EXCERPTED FROM
Pat's Story

December 1953

In the year 1945 a woman read an article about Alcoholics Anonymous. She wrote to the General Service Headquarters address in New York. A telegram from there went to the four-months-old AA group in Nacogdoches (the only one anywhere in East Texas at that time). Nacogdoches phoned their only Palestine, Texas member, who made his first Twelfth Step call on Pat, desperately sick in the hospital there.

Pat was fifty-six years old; he never took another drink of alcohol after that AA call on November 14. When he learned that he had a disease, that others suffered from it just as he did, that many had found recovery and happy sobriety through the AA therapy, he wanted that happiness too. It wasn't easy, but Pat truly wanted it.

His sister in Centerville, Texas, who had written General Service Headquarters, made room for Pat in her home ... he had long since lost his own family.

Every Thursday at noon Pat boarded a bus to Palestine, ate supper there, then went to Doc's office and rode with him to Nacogdoches for the AA meeting. They got back to Doc's home about midnight, Pat slept there, had early breakfast and then caught the eight o'clock bus back to Centerville where he arrived about noon Friday. The round trip with layovers at Buffalo both ways was about 270 miles and took twenty-four hours, but Pat thought it was worthwhile ... he didn't miss a meeting for over a year. By then Palestine held their own group on Monday nights and Pat's trip was shortened to 140 miles.

Pat's health improved, he set up his own residence, worked in his brother-in-law's general mercantile store, gradually took more responsibility, became manager and finally half owner. He returned to active church membership, became a good influence over the young people, who loved him and his ideas of clean fun, moral living, and proper dress (he was an immaculate, modern dresser). He loved football, fishing, and hunting. He was made president of the Centerville Chamber of Commerce. He became a happy, useful, Christian citizen.

In September, 1953 Centerville High School installed a new public address system, and chose Pat to announce their first football game over it. He was pleased and so glad to do it. During that pleasant event, Pat suffered a heart attack and slumped over dead.

He didn't die drunk, or miserable, or confused, or of a wet brain or in convulsions; he died happy, having known eight years of self-respect with the respect and love of all who knew him. He had carried that message of AA recovery to other drunks along the way. His children had re-discovered their father; he had spent wonderful vacations with them in Georgia and Florida at their home.

Doc B.

Palestine, Texas

Ways of Coming into AA

March 1945

M y psychiatrist maneuvered me into AA. He wrote to the clubhouse, got the secretary's name, told her about me and vice versa. But that was after we had made a bargain, following many months of psychiatric treatments. Not in a sanatorium, but in real life. Reality? I didn't know the meaning of that, and am only beginning to learn now, after twenty months in AA. You can still be holding down a job, as I was doing, and have little conception of the real world about you. The psychiatrist repeatedly told me there was no cure for alcoholism. Every few months he would gently suggest AA. While continuing to drink, I insisted there must be a cure—and rejected AA. Finally he got me there.

Pulling my feet up that long corridor leading to the main room of the clubhouse, I was going, so I thought, to my doom. I wasn't doing this of my own volition, or so my conscious mind was saying. My bargain with the psychiatrist was that I would give AA a two-week trial (his suggestion), then I could return to him and (my suggestion) he'd give me work to do to pay for future treatments.

Reaching the main room that first evening, I halted abruptly before going upstairs to the secretary. It was before the meeting hour. Men and women were standing in groups talking. I looked at them.

What followed is one of those sensations that transcends accurate description. It came with such suddenness and enveloping completeness—that feeling which said: I have come home at last.

The words repeated themselves over and over in my mind: I have come home at last. I turned and walked up the stairs with the feeling of unself-consciousness akin to that of a child—something I had never before experienced in adult life. A few days later I began to understand what my good and wise psychiatrist had known for some time: my need thenceforth lay along spiritual lines, part of which consisted in helping others—something startlingly new to me. AA, where I feel so beautifully at home, is filling that need.

Maeve S.

Club Grace

August 2007

There have been many moments of grace in the thirty-four years of my sobriety. Some were outstanding in their protection, guidance, and love. But none is more vivid than the first time I consciously experienced the miracle of AA within my own heart.

On New Year's Eve in 1973, I woke up in the alcoholic ward of a hospital in Washington, D.C. An angel from the AA desk had sent two people to my apartment in response to my drunken call of despair the day before. I was so far gone that I barely remember their Twelfth Step call that first day, but I do remember them coming to fetch me the next morning to go to the hospital. They had gone to the trouble of arranging a bed for me. Before I went down to their car, the last thing I did was to chug-a-lug a bottle of brandy. By the time I got to the hospital, I was as drunk as usual and so toxic from alcohol poisoning that the doctors decided to knock me out to keep me from convulsing. At least, that's how I remember it. I came to in the middle of the night. I was thirty years old, at a dead end, and I had no hope at all. I just wanted to make a fast end to it all.

Although I knew that I was an alcoholic, I had not called the AA desk because I wanted to get sober. I didn't believe I could get sober. I just wanted someone to come and get me. I was so terrified that I wanted some kind of help—any kind at all. I knew that AA would send someone to rescue me. I had no idea about the miracle of grace that was to begin with that phone call.

I attended my first AA meetings on the alcoholic ward of that hospital. I liked the meetings all right, but I didn't know if I intended to stay sober when I got out. I was so used to living in a nightmare of lies that I could not contact anything real inside myself to know if I was sincere. Sincere? I hardly remembered what the word meant. I was scattered and emotionally fragmented.

Nevertheless, when I was discharged, I had a copy of the Big Book and the "Where and When" schedule of meetings in the area. I took a taxi to a noon meeting in downtown D.C. before I went home.

That meeting became my home group for many years, the center of a hope, growth, and friendship I had never imagined. I still have the friends that I met there, and we remember each others' lives from when we were young. Now we are the old-timers—still striving for spiritual progress, and no longer just hoping, but certain, that AA works.

As I said, though, I didn't start out that way. For the first three months, I went to a lot of meetings and I read some of the literature—mostly so I could "talk the talk." I was so glad not to be lonely that I would have gone anywhere to not be by myself. I also didn't drink, which was so amazing that I couldn't even grasp the implications of my reprieve. But I knew I was still in danger. I knew

I wasn't for real. I hadn't even tried to work the Steps because I was too horrified at what I would have to face about myself. I still lied a lot, I was still living on the surface, but I was going to meetings. I thought I would play it out until it ended, until AA found out who I really was.

I had heard about those "who are constitutionally incapable of being honest with themselves." I was one of those people, I knew, and it was only a matter of time before the bubble burst and it would all be over, just like everything else good that had ever happened. But I didn't drink, and I kept going to a lot of meetings.

One night, I decided that I wanted to go out to dance in a club; not to drink, just to dance, and have some fun again. I called some old friends and met them downtown in a club with a live band. This is great, I thought. I looked better than I had in a long time, and I felt good. I even had a few dollars to spend. I ignored the fact that my second husband wouldn't speak to me on the telephone, and that my child was living with his father across town. I tried to ignore the heavy feeling of guilt and terror, which often broke through my thin layer of pretense that my life was getting better.

The heck with it, I thought. I'm young and I'm going out to dance!

I stood in that club and looked around for my friends. The music was loud. Everything was just as I remembered it.

But I didn't like it. I kept waiting for the old feeling of recklessness to engulf me. I wanted it to engulf me; I wanted to dive into the music and let go of my fear for a while. But I couldn't do it. I just stood there, feeling hollow and empty and out of place.

All of a sudden, I thought of the young people's meeting going on right that minute. I wished that I were there instead of at the club. Then, in a moment of timeless wonder, I realized what had happened to me. Without even knowing it, I had become a member of Alcoholics Anonymous. I was an alcoholic who was not drinking.

I actually belonged to AA and I was included in the miracle! I found what I had been looking for all my life, and I was not going to be kicked out. They wanted me. And I wanted them. In that moment, I knew I wanted the program with all my heart. My soul began to melt into tears of utter relief and gratitude. I was finally included.

I left that club and took a taxi to a meeting, just as I had when I left the hospital three months earlier. But this time I was filled with joy—I was going home, to the beginning of the rest of my sober life, one day at a time. The grace of AA had been working in me the whole time, through the meetings, through the people who brought me to meetings, who talked to me on the phone, and who were there waiting for me when I walked in, late, to the meeting that night. Most of them are still there, and so are you all, everywhere I go, every meeting I attend, every call I make. And I am here, thirty-four years later, still amazed and grateful to be included in the miracle of AA.

Jackie B.
Alexandria, Virginia

Call Before You Fall

January 2008, from PO Box 1980

E arly in my sobriety, I came home from a Saturday night AA meeting and didn't know what to do for the rest of the evening.

My wife appeared to be asleep and would not wake up, in spite of my turning on all the lights in the bedroom. I resented this, even though it was my physical abuse of her in a drunken rage that had led me to AA.

Feeling rejected, I decided to go out clubbing, telling myself I would not drink—although I had never gone out clubbing without getting drunk.

Then I remembered something I'd heard at a meeting: "Call before you fall." I picked up the phone and called an AA friend, who suggested I come to his house and talk about it.

He listened to me all night as we sat and drank coffee, although he seemed unable to come up with a solution. I began to notice light coming through his windows. It was Sunday morning, and suddenly I no longer felt a desire to party or be resentful of my wife. I thanked my friend and returned home, sober, to meet my wife coming down the stairs, asking me if I wanted breakfast.

It took me quite a few years to realize the spiritual experience I had had—God had restored me to sanity and kept me sober for another day.

That was forty-five years ago.

Ralph B.
Philadelphia, Pennsylvania

Garden Hose Sobriety

October 2006

One of the last AA meetings I attended before my self-styled graduation from Alcoholics Anonymous was at La Tuna Federal Prison. Set in a windswept desert plain, La Tuna rises up like a Spanish hacienda surrounded by razor wire and thick white walls. I saw myself supporting AA with my participation in a "hospitals and institutions" meeting that carried the message of recovery to some poor fools.

We sat in a small room behind a maze of steel doors and told our stories of recovery to a small group of uneasy, blunt-faced prison inmates. I felt depressed, washed out, tired, and lonely when we left. I returned to my Army barracks and slept uneasily beneath a prickly, stiff Army-issue blanket scented with the piney odor of Army-issue, detergent. For all my good works and good intent, this was my reward? Simply not drinking for yet another day?

Five years of AA meetings was enough, I decided. All I needed to do was just not drink, pray once in a while, and focus on my new Army life. I didn't mention any of this to my old sponsor back in New Hampshire because I knew that he would give me an earful of AA jargon: "Stop going to meetings and you'll end up drunk again."

I had better things to do than give my free time to a good cause like AA. With five years of sobriety, it was time to get busy living. Enough, already.

And live I did. I had a great time with my Army buddies. Sure, they drank a few beers, and sometimes a lot more, but I stuck with ginger ale and I was fine.

Then came the day I completed Army service and became a civilian. With the whole world in front of me, I felt giddy. Now I would chase my dream of becoming a world traveler, committed to nothing and no one. I would waste no time supporting do-good organizations like AA. I would fulfill my own sense of self-happiness. No moss for this rolling stone.

A month later, someone offered me a gin and tonic. My first reaction was fear: all that knowledge about the compulsion preceding the obsession. What the heck, no one knows me out here anyway! was my second reaction. I bolted it down and waited for the sky to crash down on my head. Nothing happened. I felt less ill at ease; a warm glow rose from my belly to my head. I took another. I became violently ill, heaving and dry heaving into the toilet, my face almost touching the water.

Eureka! I'm no longer an alcoholic, I thought. A real alcoholic could handle much, much more than two watery gin and tonics. Here I was, puking my guts out. At last! I could now drink like a normal person. All the fun I had missed!

For ten years, I tried to make up for all the fun I had let pass me by. I had fun marrying a beautiful, sensitive woman and infecting her life with my mental sickness; fun losing a beautiful new house and tens of thousands of dollars using alcoholic bad judgment; lots of fun getting fired repeatedly; big fun going into violent blackouts. I had so much fun on my last drunk that I had to bribe a couple of Mexican police officers to keep from being thrown in jail.

My wife was having so much fun that she began packing her bags to leave with our child. Good, I thought as she packed, now I can drink like I want to, without her constant nagging about how I drink too much. In a quiet voice, she told me how I had tried to strangle her to death the day before. As she was passing out, our six-year-old daughter started hitting me on the knee and crying, "Daddy, Daddy, stop! You're hurting Mommy!" She told me that I released her and passed out on the bed until evening, then left the house to drink some more.

I remembered nothing at first. Then, little fragments of the living nightmare flickered into my conscious mind, including a vivid one of my little girl desperately trying to save her mother's life. I had a vision of my life as a road that vanished into a barren, desert horizon. I was living in nothing and going nowhere fast.

Without another thought of word, I dropped to my knees and prayed for the first time in a decade. "God, I am a hopeless alcoholic," I said aloud. "I have harmed everyone who ever tried to love me. I believe you can relieve me of this insanity, as you did fifteen years ago. I fire myself from being in charge of my life and ask you to run it for me."

My wife looked at me with a mixture of contempt and wonder. She had heard my tearful repentance many times before. I would not drink for a day, a week, or a month. I would not break the living room, furniture, and on and on. She did remark that it was the first time she heard me pray to God.

An odd peace crept over me, although I felt fatigued and hungover. She could leave if she wanted to, I said. I had no right to ask her to stay, and she had every reason not to believe me. I explained that I had returned to full blown alcoholic insanity, having previously achieved six years of sobriety. I had to go back to AA, I told her, and my only hope was to abandon myself completely to God, no matter how badly I misunderstood him.

Days of sobriety turned into weeks, then into months, and then into years.

I learned from the story in the Big Book, "Acceptance Was the Answer," that I made my once cheerful and loving wife sick with my drinking. The only way to restore her to health was by listening to her as I would listen to a sick friend, that is, with respect and compassion. Today, we are closer and happier than we have ever been. We have three happy and beautiful children; two of them have never known the blight of active alcoholism.

In the years since my last bottle of cheap whiskey, I have prayed and meditated, asking, Where did I go wrong? How did I become disenchanted with AA? Was it just not having a sponsor and not going to meetings? Hadn't I done an exacting and thorough Fourth and Fifth Step that made me sweat?

At church one day, while practicing my Eleventh Step, the preacher said, "I am just a cheap, ordinary garden hose. The water that comes from me and waters your spiritual garden is not from me, it is from God. I am merely a conduit."

It dawned on me: AA never needed my "support." All my good works, like going to share the message with those guys in La Tuna, were really nothing, because I wanted to claim the credit. I wanted to be the Big Man on AA campus. That was a terrible mistake.

When I effectively practice my program, I am only a cheap dime-store garden hose carrying God's message of hope, recovery, and forgiveness. Neither Bill W. nor Dr. Bob tried hanging on to the notion that they got drunks sober. They believed they were used as agents of a Higher Power to serve his will.

When I go to a meeting today, I no longer have the delusion that I am supporting a good cause. I need AA; AA did quite well without me during my ten years of self-exile. I go to AA meetings today to hear and see how God is working. When I share at a meeting, it is not to try and "help" those poor wretches, it is because I need their help and guidance.

When I don't share at a meeting, I listen intently to let my fellow recovering drunks know that God is listening to them through me, that God is being there for them through me.

Jeff M.
El Paso, Texas

Tuning In to the Spirit

June 1986

After putting it off until there was no other viable solution to the problem, I came into AA in April 1980. I know today that each of us recovers differently, and for me a spiritual recovery was apparently the thing to be handled first. I, of course, didn't know that, nor did I engineer it. My Higher Power did.

I found myself instantly attracted to the Third and Eleventh Steps, and began to really think about and attempt to practice the suggestions contained in these Steps. But as I attempted to return to prayer, I found myself feeling awkward, empty, unable even to concentrate on what I was doing; unable to quiet the noises in my head of a thousand yesterdays and tomorrows; unable to stay in the now even for a few minutes. This realization led me to explore the possibility of using meditation to "get things quiet up there," and I picked up two paperbacks, which became my guide for the first two years. These were *Journey of Awakening*, by Ram Dass, and *What Is Meditation?*, by John White. I began to meditate a lot—whenever I could find a few minutes to sit and the willpower to clear my mind of all thoughts—just sitting in the silence and trusting what others through the ages have said: "Clear your mind of your thoughts, and God's thoughts will have room to enter."

Two years later I found myself living in New York, very much impressed with the efficiency of meditation as a tool for relieving myself of worry, depression, anxiety, and other negative emotions which I had recognized as being a large part of that which I was. I entered a Zen center, studied meditation there, and went on several of their retreats. I gained a better understanding of the dynamics of meditation as a pathway for the entrance of that reality which most people call God. After Zen, I studied yoga, and commenced to be more aware of the diverse groups of individuals the world over, all striving for a better communion with a higher source of belief, understanding, love, etc. Meditation had become, for me, the main focus of my life. I felt that AA gave me right thinking, stability, right action; and meditation gave me answers to my soul's questions of peace, love, and charity.

When I shared in AA meetings, I frequently mentioned meditation, and people would come up to me afterward with questions about how they might learn to meditate, or what I might suggest in the way of reading material or places to study. Also, when I attended Third and Eleventh Step meetings, I always wondered why the group talked about prayer and meditation rather than actually doing it together and then sharing that experience. All this eventually led me to believe that there were a sufficient number of AA members interested in meditation, but not sure how to proceed with that interest, that an active meditation workshop founded on the Eleventh Step would serve a worthwhile need.

Along with a co-chairperson, I opened the first meeting in November 1984. We began by reading the Preamble, welcoming newcomers, and then reciting the Eleventh Step: "Sought through prayer and meditation to improve our conscious contact with God as we understood Him, praying only for knowledge of His will for us and the power to carry that out." We then said that we would meditate, each in his own way, for half an hour, and then share round-robin for the following hour. We decided to add a very brief "suggestions for entering meditation" statement for the benefit of those who had never tried getting quiet and sitting in the silence. That statement went something like this: "For those of you who have never tried meditation, we suggest you sit comfortably in your chair; close your eyes and try to release any thoughts which might be running through your mind. Imagine yourself as a television set tuned to a blank channel. This channel is being left blank so that God may tune in to it and contact you through your thought system, your intuition, your feelings, or whatever. If you find it difficult to quiet your thoughts and think of nothing, then we suggest you dwell on your incoming and outflowing breath, just mentally watching it enter and leave your body; and, if it helps, mentally count those inhalations and exhalations up to ten—then backward down to one. Your mind will definitely quiet down after a few minutes."

The meetings were a great success from the very first. People were generally amazed that they could actually sit quietly and experience, without any prior practice, a sense of tremendous peace and comfort. Afterward we shared either about our experiences during the meditation or, of course, anything at all pertaining to our AA experience.

The enthusiasm and comments over having one more tool in the program have been considerable. Participants have often said that they are grateful they can now find within the AA context a place to practice their meditation which does not require any type of allegiance to a particular guru or to an unfamiliar theological belief system. This is consistent, of course, with AA's wish and suggestion that every member seek God or Higher Power, as they understand it.

Other comments have focused on the good feelings of oneness and safety that arise from doing a new thing together in a group with one's peers. Members who have become regulars to our Thursday night group often say that meditation has become a regular or indispensable part of their daily routine, and that it has brought peace and new insight to their lives. Others report that they believe they have a form of contact with a Higher Power now that they did not have before.

I am grateful to that Higher Power, which I call God, for leading me to where I am today. In five years' time, the Big Book Promises have come true for me and I have tried to dedicate my life, one day at a time, to serving the power that now guides my life and destiny.

J. M.
Manhattan, New York

SECTION THREE

Miracles, Mysteries, Synchronicities

I t may not have occurred to you, but the "click" heard by the one who pulls the trigger during a desperate, deadly Russian roulette game might be the loneliest sound in the world. You'll hear that sound yourself in the first of this amazing group of stories from AA Grapevine.

Stories? Yes, but they're also more like manifestos, confessional outpourings, reports from the uncanny world of spirit. Coming upon them in print is like experiencing their incandescent magic yourself. Reports such as these are proof that life will stop at nothing, will even shatter the boundaries of "reality," to set us free.

There are several of these mysterious stories in this section— including a man who craves booze and somehow winds up at an AA meeting instead, the appearance of an otherworldly Indian, and an uncanny recollection of one phone number when desperately needed—that of a sober AA. In one story, a heavy-metal song an alcoholic hears in jail answers all his questions. He explains: "None of the words I knew adequately described that eureka moment. It wasn't until much later that I learned that AA's good friend Carl Jung had studied this particular kind of spiritual experience and had given it a name—synchronicity. In short, there are no coincidences ... I am convinced that, had I not wondered aloud about 'the God thing,' I would not have been receptive to the response .... In my case, the god of mischief met me exactly where I was at, in a manner that I was willing and able to grasp."

We are often reminded at meetings that we are walking miracles. So should we be surprised that we find them everywhere we turn? Here are just a few.

The Voice on the Tape

January 2004

That voice, I thought. That's the woman on the tape! I was sitting in a noon meeting that I had not attended in three months. I had been the secretary but had had to give it up because of a conflict with work. A friend of mine was visiting from out of town and my sponsor was there also. We were celebrating my friend's fifteen years of sobriety with friendship, conversation, a meeting, lunch, and a trip to the ocean.

The woman whose voice I recognized was sitting in front, sharing on gratitude—the topic picked by the speaker that day. I had goosebumps as I listened to her; I began to shake, and my heart pounded in my chest. I wracked my brain trying to remember if she had said her name. Yes! She had. It was Sandy. The name matched the memory that was slowly materializing in my mind.

What I was about to experience was a sobriety dream come true. I had always wanted to meet the woman to whom that voice belonged and thank her for saving my life.

In 1987, I was trying one more time to get sober. I had just been blessed with my first DUI (two more were to follow) and a sober uncle of mine had given me the tape of an AA speaker, a woman he had heard in 1986. The tape had a black and red label with the name Sandy and a date written across it. I listened to it a few times but was frightened by some of the similarities in her story and mine, especially the part about playing Russian Roulette with a handgun and "pulling the trigger and hearing the click" and how "it was the loneliest sound because it meant one more time I had to live."

At that time in my life, that was how I was living. I would put a bullet, just one, in my .38 and go drink. When I reached "that point," I would leave whatever dive I was drinking in and drive around. (I still had a car at that time.) At some desolate spot, I would pull over, reach under the seat, pull out my gun, hold it to my head, close my eyes, and squeeze the trigger. Click. I would spin the cylinder, slam it closed, and try again. Click. I did this for a year and a half. One time it went off. The details of that scenario are not important for this story, but what I know today is there is no reason for me to be alive, except that I am supposed to be.

Sobriety was not to be mine for another year. Somehow, through all my insanity and the loss of everything—because it did get worse—I managed to keep that tape of Sandy's story.

For the first six months of my sobriety, I listened to it every day, sometimes two and three times a day. I kept thinking, If this woman made it, maybe, just maybe, I can. I listened to it until I quit shaking. I listened to it until I found a sponsor. I listened to it until I had the courage to stop listening and start talking.

Although I have had many angels in my sobriety, none was as powerful as the one whose voice I heard coming from a borrowed tape recorder for six months. Throughout the years I have played that tape for every woman I have sponsored. I have dreamed of the moment, my entire sobriety, of what was about to happen after the noon meeting on March 26, 2003.

After the meeting I turned to my sponsor and my friend and said, "I have to talk to that woman." They did not know what was happening, but they followed me down the aisle between the rows of chairs to where Sandy was leaning over, picking up her purse. I touched her arm. She did not look anything like I had pictured. She was shorter than I had imagined. She had red hair, and she was dressed all in purple.

She turned to me and smiled with a bit of a question in her eyes. I had never seen her before, and I'm sure she had never been to the meeting when I was the secretary. So, she had no idea who I was. "I recognized your voice," I managed to choke out. "I have one of your tapes. You saved my life."

Much to my surprise, she grabbed me and hugged me. I cried in her arms and told her the story of my first six months of sobriety. And I thanked her for saving my life. She reminded me of one of the promises and started to cry as well. "They do come true," she said. "'No matter how far down the scale we have gone, we will see how our experience can benefit others.' You will never know how much I needed to hear that I have made a difference in someone's life."

My sponsor and friend were witnesses to all of this, making it even more special. They, too, had tears in their eyes. My friend, who was celebrating fifteen years, exclaimed, "Well, this will keep me sober another thirty years at least!" I kept telling Sandy, "You saved my life. All of my sobriety I have wanted to thank you, and here you are!"

The day wound down. My sponsor, my friend, and I enjoyed a wonderful lunch and great recovery conversation. The ocean was spectacular, and my friend headed for home with renewed spirit for her own sobriety. After she left, I dragged out one of my boxes of AA speaker tapes. I probably have over one hundred tapes. I was going to find Sandy's tape. I hadn't listened to it in years, but I knew it was in one of two boxes. I opened the first box and sighed. The tapes were piled on top of each other with no order to them, no neat little rows. I knew I was in for a long afternoon. I reached in and pulled out the first tape my fingers touched. I turned it over: The tape had a black and red label on it and the name SANDY was written across it with a date.

Gay B.
Seaside, California

I'll Handle This Myself

May 2010

I got the call on a Thursday from my dad in Dallas that he was to undergo back surgery the following Wednesday, and he would be facing it alone. I lived in Chicago, so getting down to him at the last minute would take time and money, neither of which was in abundance for me right then.

This news was unsettling to me for a ton of reasons, but primarily because my initial emotion was sadness. My dad was always a strong, crusty kind of man with a will and a drive as hard as nails. Dad also lived like there was no tomorrow his whole life, and suddenly, at the young age of 68, his tomorrow was here.

Three years prior to this particular call, my dad, an active alcoholic, experienced a near-fatal motorcycle accident that left him with deformed legs, which should have been amputated, and a crippled spine that was starting to give way to the years of substance and physical abuse. Now here we were, together in time, he suffering his alcoholic consequences and me in my sixth year of sobriety. I struggled with the influx of feelings that came as a result of his consequences crashing into my sobriety.

I looked at this trip as something I was called to do from my Higher Power, so I set out for the two-day drive with little money and my 18-year-old daughter Lindsey, who was on summer break.

The day we left was hot and sunny and there was nothing ahead of us but hundreds of miles and thousands of thoughts. I quickly settled into thinking about my dad. My dad as I grew up, my dad as I reached womanhood, my dad as I got married, my dad as I had children, my dad as I went through a divorce, my dad as I suffered through extremely tough financial times ... my dad, my dad, my dad. As I went on with these thoughts, the dark feelings they created started to take hold of valuable space in my head. I started to rekindle old resentments, resentments that I was sure I had let go of the first year I was sober.

This was my dad, who was hardly around when I was growing up, and when he was, never expressed a desire to be available for me, physically or emotionally; who, as I started to mature, never had a positive, kind word of praise or acknowledgement to give me; who, because he did not like my wedding plans, chose not to attend my wedding; who, as I had my children, never once called to see how we were or express any loving emotion.

About four hours and 280 miles into the thoughts, I realized that for some reason I felt it was OK to resurrect these long-forgotten resentments and play with them for a while. Play I did. I played all the way past Memphis before I realized how awful I was making myself feel. I quickly regained my sober bearings and had a chat with myself.

I said, "Self, you can continue to play with these dangerous thoughts, and become so miserable by the time you get to Dallas that you will be of no use to yourself or anyone else, or, you can let these old, rutty resentments go." I chose to try and let them go for the sake of my sanity and my heart. I drove for 100 miles outside of Memphis listening to music and singing.

I said nothing, I called no one and I prayed for nothing. I made the executive decision to handle this weird experience with my old resentful self—bad idea.

I passed a billboard ad for tequila and I remembered my love for tequila back in the day. At first I gave it no thought, for about 50 miles. Then, bam! Something that had not crossed my mind for six years was flying around in my head looking for a place to land: the thought to have a drink. After all, I deserved it, I told myself.

Crazy, I thought, as I drove a little faster. Maybe if I accelerated to a comfortable 20 miles over the speed limit, I could get further away from myself and the thoughts that were hauntingly familiar and relentless.

I said nothing, I called no one and I prayed for nothing. I decided I would still handle this myself.

We checked into a hotel in Hot Springs, Ark., our destination for a night of rest before the final six-hour drive to Dallas the next day.

While my daughter and I were freshening up for dinner, my thoughts raced. Who would ever know if I just had one little drink when my daughter wasn't looking? I could excuse myself to go to the restaurant restroom and sneak off to the bar; she would never know! Or I could finish dinner, and then stop at the store across from the hotel and buy a little something for as soon as she fell asleep! Even though the thoughts were powerful, I had the presence of mind to know I was in trouble, big trouble.

I was still determined to handle this myself. I said nothing, called no one and prayed for nothing.

We finished dinner and even though I was still thinking about drinking, I left the restaurant sober—well, "dry," at least. Nothing about how I was thinking was sober. I was so squirrely that I knew I had to figure something out or I was going to drink.

I still said nothing, called no one and prayed for nothing.

There was a gas station right before our hotel and I decided that what I needed was a cigar—that was the ticket! I had quit smoking cigarettes three years before, and I knew that if I bought a pack of cigarettes I would be right back at those the same way I would be right back at a bottle of vodka after one sip. A cigar? I hated cigars, and that would take away the icky feeling I had. I just knew it. I ran into the store and bought one. Lindsey was stunned as I lit the thing, but she sat in silence at first. Then she asked, "Mom, isn't smoking that cigar some kind of a relapse for you?"

"No!" I curtly exclaimed, as I took a long hot drag off that nasty thing. Who did she think she was, talking to me about "relapsing" on a cigar? Two drags were all I needed before I tossed it out the window and proceeded to go back to the safety of my hotel—which did not have a bar. A good night's sleep was what I needed.

I said nothing, I called no one, I prayed for nothing. As the nasty taste of the cigar lingered in my mouth, I realized how close I was to the edge. I felt real fear for the first time.

My daughter and I headed to our room. I felt that if I could just get into bed I would make it to the morning sober. I also realized that what I had done on the road that day—not asking for any help from anyone, by way of a call or a prayer—was to allow my disease to start driving the bus again. I had played with dangerous resentments, and when those became too uncomfortable, I gave in to my disease further and started playing with the romance of the drink.

I took a hot bath, relieved that I had made it and handled the crazies without drinking. Whew; that was close. As I stepped up against my side of the bed to pull back the covers, my bare foot touched something cold. I yelped as I stepped back, and my daughter jumped away from her side simultaneously. We share a fear of bugs and that was the first thing that went through both of our heads without a word being exchanged.

"What is it, Mom? A bug?" she exclaimed.

"I don't know!" I dropped to one knee to pick up whatever the cold metal thing was.

As I reached past the bed skirt and into the darkness underneath the bed, my finger went right to it. I picked up the object and held it up to the light. I was in awe and astonishment—smack dab in the middle of experiencing a spiritual awakening like no other. The cold metal object was a tarnished 24-hour AA coin!

I couldn't say anything and my daughter just stood there looking at me, waiting for me to say something. Although she had no idea what I had in my hand, there was an unspoken awareness that we were sharing a moment of divinity. The tears welled up in my eyes. Suddenly I realized that God was doing for me what I could not do for myself, and he had been all day long! I have had experiences that could only be explained as spiritual awakenings or miracles before, but nothing quite as astounding as this. The best part of this miracle was that I had a witness!

I immediately started to worry about the poor person who'd lost this coin, and I hoped they hadn't relapsed. But I quickly let that go, thanked God profusely and settled into the bed, coin in my hand, for what turned out to be one of the most restful sleeps I'd had in quite a while. I slept with God because of God!

Wendi V.
Crystal Lake, Illinois

The Resentment With No Name

April 2007

When I finally gave up and begged God for help, I had been dry and going to AA meetings for seven years. I wasn't happy, joyous, or free; angry, scared, and losing hope was more like it. I also had a big resentment.

I'd tried the geographical cure—I moved from the Seattle area, where a judge had correctly diagnosed my alcoholism and directed me to AA—to south Texas, and then to Alaska. I kept thinking that adventure and excitement would be my answer. But in Alaska, my credit card, which I used to escape from the pain of my actions, expired. Because I had traveled so much, the new one hadn't caught up with me. I couldn't run. So I had to feel my life, and it felt scary. I remembered what I'd heard in a meeting, "What do you have to lose?" It was obvious, even to me, that my way wasn't working. So, one day out at the Soldotna Airport, I fell on my knees and said, "God, help me." And I really meant it.

I was willing to go to any lengths. Within a few days, I got a sponsor and started working the Steps.

John M. patiently worked with me. When I got to Step Four, he told me to write down the "people, institutions, or principles" that made me angry. One of the first people I put down was the commanding officer in my U.S. Navy aviation detachment. I couldn't remember his name.

My thinking went like this: I was over in Vietnam risking my life for my country (actually, I was getting three squares a day, a shower, and my own bed every night, with little risk of attack on my aircraft carrier). When my brother died, this "lifer" (a derogatory term) refused to give me emergency leave to go home and comfort my family. So, I certainly felt wronged. Wasn't I a victim? Didn't life suck? Why wasn't life more fair?

John told me that even if I couldn't find the people I needed to make amends to, I should change my attitude so that I would be willing to make the amend if God ever presented the opportunity.

Throughout the years, I persevered in cleaning up the wreckage of my past.

I traveled to my father's grave and made peace with him. With the help of AA's principles, I no longer run, and I don't owe anyone any money. As I learned to work the principles of the program, other parts of my life began to improve. One day in 1992, in Anchorage, Alaska, I was asked to split a pitch with another member at a Sunday morning meeting. I met Stu, the other speaker. After the meeting, we decided to go out for breakfast.

As Stu and I talked, we shared about our drinking: "I did a lot of my drinking in the Navy," Stu said. "Oh, yeah? Me, too," I replied. "I was on a carrier at Yankee Station in 1968." "Really? Me, too." "I was an enlisted man in an aviation squadron on the F.D.R." "Oh yeah? Which one?"

I named the squadron. Stu piped up and said, "I was your commanding officer!" Afterward, I was able to tell him my story, and how working the Steps over four years had helped relieve me of my resentment against him.

The resentment-causing encounter between Stu and I occurred in 1968. I went on to drink another sixteen years and, when I was really feeling down, I would dredge up my resentment against a man whose name I couldn't remember. But in 1992, God brought us together in an AA meeting halfway around the world. My resentment was gone and we were both sober. What happened that morning proved to me that there is a God, that he loves me, and that his schedule is better than anything I can think up.

When I follow the "blueprint for living" in the Big Book, I get a life that is happy, joyous, and free.

When I first came to Alcoholics Anonymous, I couldn't see how the Steps would help me with my problems. But today, I no longer fight or question this program. Ever since I honestly did Step Three, the evidence of a loving God is everywhere, and each day I try to work the discipline outlined in Step Eleven into my life. I'm one of the fortunate ones.

Steve E.
Paso Robles, California

Jackpot

May 2006

S trange thing about a casino—upon entering, the noise and clamor seem normal and in no time, it seems your body needs these chaotic surroundings. Lights flashing, eyes fixated on machines and, everywhere, alcohol. Looking back, it's little wonder that this all comes in one neat package.

In all my years of drinking, I cannot remember one time that I possessed more clarity than the day I stood in a casino in Laughlin, Nevada, overlooking the Colorado River. My high school friend and I had made our way there from Las Vegas, and he'd decided to place a few bets on the football games being played that weekend.

Enshrined forever in my memory is his one request, made as the midday sun shone through the giant picture windows behind the casino bar. He asked that I not begin to drink until that evening. Just for this one day, would I wait until we'd had dinner and then we could head "out on the town"? Who could blame him for cringing at the prospect of once again seeing his friend being drunk and wiped out by late afternoon?

I agreed with his request, with nothing but the best of intentions. As he walked away, I turned and admired the view of the river cutting a majestic path through the dry lands of southern Nevada. These windows were directly behind a small bar that had several bar stools in front. All were full, except for one seat in the middle. Room enough for one more broken promise.

In the less than ten minutes that my friend was away, I had three beers; I was set. No more lack of familiarity, insecurity, or low self-esteem. In this town, there were now only equals, and I was the first amongst them.

Perhaps the most telling story of that day wasn't the victory of my compulsion to drink; it was my friend's lack of surprise. It's mystifying how the people around us adjust so quickly and have little difficulty in accepting the most minimum standard of behavior.

The rest of our day in Laughlin was predictable, as was the whole trip. My drinking, followed in short order by drunkenness, self-centered behavior, and then remorse and misery. In a few days, we found ourselves leaving Nevada for Toronto. Back home to the void that was the life I had carefully constructed.

It was the typical "red eye" flight, and it wasn't long before just about everyone had fallen asleep or blacked out. All, that is, except me. I was in the position that only an alcoholic can truly appreciate. Not dead, not alive, and wishing for neither.

I'd hit that limit where alcohol just didn't work despite my best efforts throughout the day. I can't think of anything more terrifying than a dry alcoholic sitting on an airplane in the middle of the night while everyone else is asleep. God only knows, we're lonely enough.

I looked out the window across the aisle at the blackness that seemed a metaphor for my life. Moving along, but completely unchanging in appearance. Time passing with seemingly nothing accomplished.

It wasn't always like this. There had been promises and dreams. Achievements and a career set on the right path. At every crossroads on my journey through life, I'd found the turn. Fueled by alcoholism, more than alcohol itself, I always strove with vigor to find a way to fail.

If I could have somehow managed it, I would have stayed on that plane forever. At least the reality of the life I'd left behind would not await me at the airport terminal. But land it did and there it was, powerlessness and unmanageability. The cornerstones of a life operating on the principle of "self-will run riot." Also waiting, the loyal shield from reality, alcohol.

Before long, I was safely enshrined in my favorite basement chair situated directly in front of the television. Beer glass in hand, I resumed my journey into hell. I've heard people speak of alcoholics not having to go to hell since they've already been there. Being downstairs, at least I was moving in the right direction every time I headed for alcoholic oblivion.

I'd drink every day, living off the money accumulated from a severance package from my last employer. Who could conceive of anything worse than a practicing alcoholic with money to burn and nowhere to be on any given day?

The pattern repeated itself each and every day. Drink and then pass out, only to awaken in the middle of the night to endure the insomnia and unspeakable loneliness that only the alcoholic can fully comprehend.

On those nights, I remember glancing at the wooden desk directly across from my bed. On it lay that now familiar blue book. It was thick and had never been opened.

It had been left there by my twin sister sometime before. A year, two maybe—it had been on that desk for a long time. When I drank, I'd have to put it in the desk and close the drawer. Its presence in such times was much too uncomfortable. Yet, in my blackout phase I'd reach for it and then, upon coming to, there it would sit on the desk, overshadowing everything else within range.

My twin had found AA several years before. I'd joke with her as she left to go to those strange meetings. Not so much to denigrate her, or the way of life she'd found, as to avoid any possible recognition that I might need to follow in her footsteps.

I often asked God to help me, yet those prayers had seemed to go unanswered. I would later thank him for the apparent silence. His unconditional love for me allowed the time I needed to suffer so that, when the truth was found, I would have the ears to hear, the arms to embrace, and the heart to hold.

My Higher Power gave to me in my twin sister the only message I would ever be able to understand. The only words I could comprehend, and the single truth that no alcoholic in search of peace could ignore. He gave me an example, someone who had walked my road and somehow managed to change.

On a cold Saturday night, I picked up the phone and called her through the haze of one more drunken evening. She told me of a meeting the next night and I declined. Too busy. What about Monday? Too busy. Tuesday? Okay. She passed me to a man who would become my sponsor and the arrangements were made.

The following days were full of remorse for the call, for my life, and for the desperate world I had built for myself. But, in the moment I'd made the call, I had conceded my powerlessness over one thing in my life and begged of my Higher Power the help that would soon come in waves.

Standing on the street outside my home, I watched as the car approached. The man welcomed me and explained that I should try to keep an open mind and maybe this place was for me.

The rest of the story is much the same for many of us. Those who carried the message to me that night embraced me. I heard a man speak and my eyes welled with tears. This was the first time in my life I'd heard someone talk of his life in a manner not unfamiliar to me. I felt a part of something. I was no longer alone.

Four days later, I went to an open meeting at my sister's group. She got up that night and received her five-year medallion. This recognition of her five years of continuous sobriety was honoring a milestone in her journey that had actually passed four days earlier.

Same birthday, same dry date. Some may say coincidence, but I prefer Providence. On March 26, God willing, we'll celebrate together.

We grew up together surrounded by much hardship and often tragic circumstances. We developed the same spiritual, mental, and physical ailment that robbed us of life. Yet, five years apart, we found that there was also a common solution.

The program of Alcoholics Anonymous has given us a road map that shows us how to live our lives—one that, with God's grace, we will take forever, five years apart, but only one day at a time.

Michael G.
North York, Ontario

Between Grace and Hope

March 2008

was born between grace and hope. Mrs. Grace and Mrs. Hope, that is—two women who lived on either side of my house. When I turned ten, I joined a gang and started drinking wine. Within two years, I had been arrested numerous times and I was looking at ending up in the State Correctional System—which is a code word for "youth prison."

I received a little grace about that time because I was saved from going to the kids' joint and I broke away from the gang. I stopped drinking for a few years. My new obsession became to fit in and to be liked. But by the seventh grade, I returned to alcohol. At that time, it served me well. When I became a senior in high school, I had achieved my goals without going to jail or prison.

I was elected to be my high school's Student Body President, Citizen of the Year, and a host of other awards. Only alcohol gave me the feeling of being connected to my family. But when the effect wore off, it was back to alienation, desperation, and a very lonely existence.

Alcohol made it possible for me to perform and play all the parts needed to be popular and successful. Yet, I felt separated from everyone and everything.

In college, I became a full-blown alky and had to drink in order to operate in the world of the living. I graduated with a flat C average and was plagued with mania and depression.

I courted and married a lovely and bright young lady—the head cheerleader of our college. I was fully intoxicated when I met her. It was my way of coping even when professing my love. We got pregnant when she was nineteen and I was twenty-one. Nine months later, I was a dad to a beautiful little girl. A month after our daughter was born, I was on my way to Vietnam, where alcohol became even more plentiful. I could get a quart of booze for a buck, and beer at the enlisted clubs was a quarter a bottle.

I was arrested while I was in the Navy because I failed to report back in time. The charges were dropped and I was let go with a warning and no leave for two weeks. One night, while off the coast of Vietnam, I got blind drunk. I remember trying to get from the boatswain's locker to my rack (bed). I was outside, in pitch darkness, slipping and sliding. I could have fallen overboard and no one would have known.

There are countless other disasters where for some reason or another I was spared by grace. I drove drunk many times with my wife and kids in the car. Once, I left my four-year-old son in the car by himself, asleep. I told myself that I could sneak into the bar, get some booze, and be out before he woke up. It was eight in the morning and I had to have a drink. When I returned from the bar, I didn't have any idea how long I had been inside. I found my little son crying with both hands on the window. The thought of what could have happened filled me with shame and guilt. That was the beginning of the end.

Around this time, I got drunk again and for no apparent reason I got very angry with my wife. Without warning, I ran up to her and, in front of her family and mine, I spit in her face. I had become a monster! A few days later, we were on our way back home to the Northwest. She told me not to speak to her. After driving for two days, we got home. Once there, she asked me to listen to her very carefully. She said: "I do not know if I will ever forgive you for what you did and for what you have become. I do not respect you and I think the love that I had for you is gone."

A few months later, she asked me to move out. She, along with our son and daughter, stayed in the brand-new home we had just purchased. We were not able to stay married because, as she put it, there was nothing left to put together.

At the same time, I finished my course work for my doctorate and passed all my exams. I had been promoted several times and I was interviewing at some of the best universities in California for excellent positions in my field.

I was starting to get physically ill from alcohol poisoning. I was caught in a whirlwind of alcoholism and I had no idea how to get free. I approached a colleague regarding alcoholism on an academic level. I told him that I was interested in how alcoholics went about getting sober and staying sober. He told me that the best way was to go to Alcoholic Anonymous, because that way you didn't have to do it by yourself and you never had to do it alone again. I concluded that the poor man lacked social skills and that was why he went to AA meetings—so he didn't have to be alone.

Soon, I was arrested for drunk driving and lost my license for six months. I felt like my world was coming apart. All I could do was drink and then use other drugs to help curb my drinking. It was a miracle that I did not end up in prison because I was involved with some drug dealers. Again, grace spared me. One of my friends got arrested, but brokered a deal to stay out of prison. Another pal took a forty-five revolver, shot himself in the mouth, and died. It seemed there was doom everywhere.

But a very strange thing happened next. Today, it almost seems unbelievable. An old Mexican Indian came into town looking for me. Although he did not speak English, he got the nurses to call me at the university to come to the hospital where he had faked a heart attack. When I got there, he had an instant recovery, and off we went. He knew I was a psychologist, but how he knew about my alcoholism is somewhat of a mystery. He told me he was there to save my life and that it was imperative that I remove alcohol and drugs from my life. He stayed with me and my son for two days while I went through withdrawal. On the last night, he told me that I would have a window of opportunity to get well, and that I must seize that opportunity. Then he disappeared. I looked for him in our small town but I could not find him. I wondered what the window of opportunity would look like.

A few months later, I was offered a position in southern California and I accepted it. While there, I had another one of those nights that turned into morning as I drank another bottle of wine—by myself. I decided to call my aunt. As I was crying and feeling sorry for myself, she said something that slapped me hard across the face. She said, "You are responsible for your condition—nobody else." Then she said good-bye and hung up the phone. It all became crystal clear—I could not stay sober by myself. I needed help. I called AA immediately. This was my moment of clarity and the window of opportunity that the old Mexican Indian told me about.

When I called AA, they said a man would call me. A few minutes later, a total stranger called and said, "My name is Bill and I am an alcoholic. Would you like to go to a meeting at noon?" I said, "Yes." I went to my first meeting with Bill and then he bought me a Big Book and took me to lunch. He has been my sponsor since that day—over thirty years ago. I have been sober since March 23, 1977.

Some years later, Bill asked me, "What are the odds of a Jew from New York City and a Mexican from Anaheim, California, meeting and becoming the closest of friends?" Thirty years later, we both knew it was the grace of a merciful God and the miracle of AA.

As far as I can tell, AA is full of grace, but, since we cannot give away what we do not have, it is imperative to work all of the Twelve Steps, to respect and honor the Twelve Traditions, and to practice these principles to the best of our human capabilities in all of our affairs.

My two kids are now university professors. My daughter is married and I have three grandsons who have only known their grandfather as a sober member of society. I have been married to my wife, a sober member of AA, for twenty-two years. She has over twenty-five years of sobriety and we celebrate the grace of God one day at a time, each day of our lives.

Santiago E.
Laguna Niguel, California

Sunshine of the Spirit

June 2006

I f you love everybody in AA, you ain't makin' enough meetings!"

That's just one of the borrowed bromides Tommy Sunshine crowed from his folding chair in the back of the church hall. He had that odd talent of quoting lines he'd heard in the rooms and making them his own. Even if he gave full credit to their authors, you somehow still imagined the lines originating from him. My old man did the same thing—made pocketed phrases his own by the intensity with which he delivered them:

"If you're gonna do a job, do it right or don't do it at all!" "God helps those who help themselves!" "Less jaw work and more paw work!"

When I was drinking, I could never do any job right, so I didn't even try. As far as helping myself, how could I when I didn't even know I needed it? By the time I made it to AA, I might as well have had paws, considering how much time I spent crawling on all fours from the bed to the bathroom and beyond.

I got sober in Washington Heights—that's where I met Tommy Sunshine, facetiously nicknamed because of his unapologetic surliness. He chaired The Bridge meeting so long that, at his memorial service, the pastor referred to the room downstairs as his ministry. In a way, Tom was The Bridge during the tough times when membership was meager, attendance spotty, and service a dirty word. Maybe that accounted for his orneriness or maybe he was just a product of his generation, one in which a tough guy veneer (and heavy drinking history) was usually a preexisting condition.

My dad might have had a few years on Tom but he was cut from the same cloth. There was one big difference though—Tom found the way out and my father didn't.

Like my father, Tom didn't make suggestions—he made threats. It wasn't tough love, it was ruthless. I started avoiding him the way I had my father in the old days. But then, one Thursday night, a few years into sobriety, something remarkable happened. I was chairing a meeting at my home group and Tom made a crack about how I wasn't doing something "right" (in other words, the way he'd do it). I was on the verge of losing it, like I always did when I was criticized. Ready to storm out or start crying; you know, crash and burn—my usual M.O. But I didn't do any of those things. Instead, I barked back:

"Look, give me a break! I've had a rough week. I'm tired. I'm doing the best I can. I'm chairing this meeting the only way I know how to chair it. I don't tell you what to do at The Bridge so don't tell me what to do here!"

Then, the miracle. Tommy Sunshine didn't flip out or go off on me. He just stood there, grinning from ear to ear, and crooned, "Thanks for sharing."

Just like that, we were friends. He wasn't my father or my boss or my Higher Power, he was just a sober alcoholic doing the best he could with what he had.

And so was I.

I'm not saying all was smooth sailing with Tommy Sunshine after that little epiphany. He continued to act as the unofficial sponsor or drill sergeant I never asked for, and we would get into it from time to time, locking horns at business meetings, or arguing such salient issues as bagels versus hoagies for the holidays. When I watched other newer-than-I newcomers get frustrated and angry with him, I waited for the day when they would make their stand and see what I had seen—the love behind the bitching and barking.

Hearing Tom qualify brought a lot home as well. From getting into the Navy on a Chinese laundry ticket, to drinking alcohol from the ships' compasses, to directing traffic with his pants down on Fort Washington Avenue, his was a wild story.

He got sober on a ruse—bringing a worse-off-than-he drinking buddy to the VA hospital rehab and then taking his place when the pal reneged. In a few short months, he went from living in a box under the bridge to doing service at The Bridge, helping many of the sick and suffering homeless drunks he had once walked among. I thought my story was lightweight compared to his. Until he heard me speak and told me how much identification he had with the pain and the anger and isolation, with having to put on a show in order to survive out there.

I love the part in the "Twelve and Twelve" where it says that we are people who probably wouldn't mix. Tom and I couldn't have been more different. I had a college education. He did not. He had run his own business. I had not. I was a man who called myself an artist. He was an artist who called himself a man. But our bond was inevitable and indissoluble: We both had alcoholic fathers. We both were alcoholic sons.

Tom's father never changed. But Tom did—twice. The first time by getting sober, turning his life around, reclaiming his family, and becoming a vibrant and productive member of our fair city. The second change was no less profound, and happened when he became ill.

In a few short years, I watched his transformation from bleeding deacon to elder statesman coincide with the diagnosis and progression of a cancer that first claimed his voice, then his freedom, and finally his life. Gradually, the petty squabbles about doing things this way or that way dissolved. His ego retreated, his whole tone softened, his warmth became palpable. And when the last wall had crumbled, there he was, the real Tommy Sunshine, with humility and grace as his mantle. The sicker he got, the harder he worked the program, the more he practiced these principles in his affairs. A handyman by trade, he was a power of example to us all in facing, with dignity and sobriety, his last odd job on the planet.

There's something that happens in AA, between members of this Fellowship, that I have never felt anywhere else. I sense the presence of a Higher Power I cannot understand or explain. The moment of silence before the Serenity Prayer is one of those times. Another is sitting with a fellow alcoholic during a tough spell. Not because you know what to do or say, but because you know in your heart it's where you need to be, in order to give what you can. And, every time, what you get is always so much more.

The last time I saw Tom at the hospital, he gave me something I never even knew I needed. He helped settle an old debt, quell a long carried guilt. A guilt undiminished by counting days or years, untouched by Fourth and Fifth Steps, circumvented by therapy and counseling and sharing. A guilt intact because I had never told anyone, because I had stayed as sick as my secret. And though Tommy Sunshine was oblivious to the whole business, he was the one who set me free.

Twenty-five years ago, my father lay dying in a hospital bed. Despite his critical condition, and not surprisingly, he was still calling some of the shots. Most significant was his refusal to be catheterized and his insistence on using the small plastic urinal kept at his bedside.

On my last visit, he was more disoriented than usual and unable to use the urinal cup without assistance. Although I had braced myself with a few stiff ones at the bar next door, I was still not prepared for the nurse's suggestion that he might be more comfortable if I helped him.

I flashed back to being a kid, how fiercely private my dad had been about his body, slamming the bathroom door shut angrily, dangerously.

I made more than enough desperate excuses: I was too shook up, he wouldn't want me to see him like this, on and on. There was some truth there but, in the end, I just couldn't deal with his helplessness, his body, his death, any of it.

As my brother-in-law stepped up to the plate to do the deed, I slipped out into the hall, then back to the bar for more "courage."

My last call on Tommy Sunshine was a quiet one. He could no longer speak, only point. Yet, his pointing seemed to have some voice still in it—pushy and commanding—like the old days of chairing meetings and twelfth-stepping newcomers at The Bridge: "You! Sit there! You! Read this!"

As I got ready to leave, Tom held up his hand. He pointed to the plastic urinal clipped to the railing of the bed and nodded toward the bathroom in the corner of the room. I balked.

"You want me to … ?"

He nodded and began rolling his hands and arms in a circular motion, imitating the wheelchair and giving me my unspoken marching orders. Now!

I did not put up a front, or fan my fear, or excuse myself. Any reservations or hang-ups I might have had were clearly beside the point. I looked into the eyes of my friend, who had loved and annoyed me into sobriety, and saw that all he needed was this last little thing. It wasn't about me this time, it was about first things first. So I grabbed the damned cup, rolled the old coot into the John, and helped him do what he had to do.

I find it hard to describe my gratitude. To AA and to Tommy Sunshine, who forced me, in a way, in his way, to make that amend to my old man. To do the next right thing, no matter how difficult or unnatural it might have, seemed to me. Because, when you come right down to it, it was all perfectly natural, just one alcoholic helping another.

My father and I tried our best to love each other and didn't always succeed. I know that Tommy Sunshine felt the same way about his dad. In the end, Tom and I were the lucky ones. In getting sober, we actually learned a little bit about how to love, and how to be loved. I like to think we made our fathers proud without them even knowing it.

I've met so many amazing people in this amazing Fellowship throughout the years. I do my best to welcome edgy newcomers and to be tolerant of grumpy old-timers. I'm getting better at giving people a fair shake, learning to hold off on quick judgments, and not taking inventories other than my own. But, to be rigorously honest, I must admit that I don't love everybody in AA.

According to Tommy Sunshine, I must be making enough meetings

Richard H.
New York, New York

A Heartbreaker

June 2006

When I was sober for three years, I decided to move from Pennsylvania to Florida. My sponsor asked me if I had cleaned my side of the street and made amends to the best of my ability and knowledge. My answer was yes. Then I asked myself the ultimate question, which was whether or not I wanted to shovel snow anymore, and that answer was no, so I moved to Florida.

I had been in Florida four months and was feeling pretty good about everything. So, I decided to take a long weekend, take another look at my Eighth and Ninth Steps to make sure that I had cleaned my side of the street, head to Key West, and spend some relaxing time on the beach. Little did I know that there are no beaches in Key West (I lived on the west coast.)

As I traveled across the state, a young lady's name from the past popped into my mind. I thought about how I hadn't treated her well in high school. I used to tell her that I would pick her up for a date, and instead I would end up getting drunk with my buddies. I thought about how, throughout my life, this girl's name would pop up and, every once in a while, I would get drunk, find her phone number, and call her in the middle of the night. Or I would call her mother to find out where she was. Her name was Paula.

After driving awhile, I got closer to the east coast. I found a radio station that played tunes from the fifties, sixties, and seventies. To my delight, one of my favorite songs started to play—"Hey, Hey, Paula." I chuckled to myself about the coincidence, and continued my journey to Key West.

When I arrived, I checked out some of the sites, but couldn't find the darned beach, so I decided to turn around and head back home. As I got closer to Miami, I turned on the radio again and guess what song started playing? That's right, "Hey, Hey, Paula."

Now, thinking of this girl and hearing that song twice in one day, I said, "Okay, God, I get the message." I did not know where she lived. After all, it had been over twenty years. I did, however, know where her mother lived. So, I did what was taught to me in the program of AA. I wrote her a letter.

I wrote that I believed that I had broken her heart in high school and that I was working on changing my life. I wrote that I hoped she was doing well.

I sent the letter to her mother's address, with no return on the outside (if there had been a return address, her mother might not have given it to her). But my address was inside the letter itself, just in case.

She wrote back. I opened the letter, scared of what I might find. It began, "You didn't break my heart in high school. You crushed it."

Now I wondered if I should read the rest of the letter, but I did. She was glad to hear from me and said that it was okay to write again. So I did. That was August 1998.

The following Thanksgiving, God gave me the opportunity to see someone I hadn't seen in twenty-three years. Paula was going to be in Orlando with her daughter's high school band. We had a fantastic time getting to know each other again.

Paula worked at a university in Pennsylvania and still had a few years before thinking about retirement, so we stayed in touch long distance for the next few years. As we communicated, we discovered things about one another.

She learned about how I had found God and myself through the Twelve Steps. I told her how I'd used the Steps in my life to solve any problem and uncover the fears that kept me away from the sunlight of the spirit, and how I used the Steps to discover that inside each of us there is a God-given goodness.

I learned that she, too, had had difficulties. She had survived cancer not once, but twice. She'd survived bankruptcy and her father's death, and had struggled with a drug-addicted fifteen-year-old son.

What was my response to these dilemmas? Trust God, clean house, help others. As a result of practicing the Twelve Steps, many have been able to meet the difficulties of life. Practicing the Steps can be more than a road to sobriety for problem drinkers. It can be a way to happy and effective living for many, alcoholic or not.

I witness this on a daily basis because, you see, in January 2003, I asked Paula if she was tired of shoveling snow and wanted to come to the sunny south to live with me, and her answer was yes. We were married on May 8, 2004.

Cub W.
Punta Gorda, Florida

Serenity Graffiti

October 2008, from PO Box 1980

Sometimes my Higher Power needs to get my attention.

One sunny afternoon, I was rushing from place to place, late for my next appointment. The lady in the car in front of me was taking her sweet time. Didn't she know what a hurry I was in? My temper reared its ugly head, and I started yelling at her to hurry up. Thank God, my window was closed and she couldn't hear me.

By the time she got through the intersection, a train ahead was blocking our progress. As my childish yelling continued, a train car rolled past with the following message spray-painted four feet high on its side: "E-Z DUZ IT."

I burst out laughing, and thanked my HP for his sense of humor and perfect timing. Needless to say, the rest of my day went a lot better.

Jeff W.
Redcliff, Alberta

EXCERPTED FROM

The Sounds of Sobriety

January 1999

G od's hands can be seen in every act of my life. Two years ago I was driving at night from my mother's home to mine, listening to a Grapevine tape ("Sonidos de Sobriedad"), when I was assaulted by a gang who took my car and my personal belongings, including credit and ATM cards, put me in the trunk, and drove around the city for an hour. I was scared, since I didn't know what they were going to do with me. I had seen their faces and I didn't have too much hope. But I heard the tape running all the time and serenity came to me. This was a situation I was not able to change, so I had to accept it.

To my surprise, the guys changed. They seemed to be more concerned about my comfort and decided to drop me in a deserted place and drive away. It is my belief that the tape changed their mood.

The first thing I did when I got home was to open my *Daily Reflections* book at random and I received from God the message of March 17, which corresponds to page 111 of the "Twelve and Twelve" and is titled "MYSTERIOUS WAYS": "... out of every season of grief or suffering, when the hand of God seemed heavy or even unjust, new lessons for living were learned, new resources of courage were uncovered, and ... finally, inescapably, the conviction came that God does move in a mysterious way His wonders to perform."

Marcelo R.
Bogotá, Colombia

Tip From a Bartender

December 2007

I n early sobriety, I had a hard time grasping the idea that God had been watching and waiting for me to reach out to him throughout all the years of my drinking. It was beyond my comprehension that God could care about one little drunk.

Then, barely four months into my recovery, my Higher Power convinced me otherwise.

My sponsor told me that if I entertained the argument, in my head, about whether or not to take a drink, I wouldn't win the argument. Alcoholism would win every time. Although I heard him, I did not internalize it as a fact.

At four months sober, I had to make a business trip from my home in Atlanta to Washington, D.C. My plane had not even cleared the ground at the Atlanta airport when the argument in my head began: Over 600 miles from home. No one in Washington knows I'm in AA. I could drink tonight and by the time I come home Friday, it would all be out of my system. It would be easy. No one would know—except me.

The argument continued, relentlessly, throughout the flight. During the cab ride from the airport to a luxury hotel in Capitol Hill, I barely heard a word the driver said. The argument in my head was too loud, too relentless.

As I entered the huge atrium lobby of the hotel, a familiar sound captured my attention. It was the sound of laughter and the tinkling of glasses. The voices were still there, saying, No one will know. Go ahead. Live it up!

In less than ten minutes, I checked into the hotel, dumped my luggage in the room, and took the elevator back to the lobby. I stood for several minutes at the entrance of the bar as the argument played in my head, loudly and emphatically. My sponsor's admonition: "If you entertain the argument about whether to drink or not to drink, you'll lose," was overcome by those voices. I lost.

I walked into the bar and sat down. The bartender came over, looked at me several seconds, and then said, "Hi, pal. How about a soda?" I stared at him. He continued, "I figured, by that lapel pin you're wearing, that's what you'd want."

I had forgotten to remove the little round lapel pin with a triangle from my sport coat—my AA pin! He knew what it meant. He placed a soda in front of me and moved on to serve other patrons. Then he returned to stand in front of me, again.

"You don't have any business in here, do you?" he asked with a faint smile.

"No," I replied meekly.

"Where you belong is three blocks down the street, upstairs over the furniture store. There's a meeting in twenty minutes. Get out of here," he said, motioning toward the door.

I went to that AA meeting, and, before turning in for the night, I did two more things. I walked back into that bar and thanked the angel in the shape of a bartender for saving my life. Laughingly, he replied, "You weren't in too much danger. I saw you standing in the door for so long that I thought you were looking for someone. But when you sat down, I saw that lapel pin and the anxious look on your face. I knew what you were up to. There was no way in hell you were going to get a drink out of me!"

He went on and told me that he was a substitute bartender, only working that night.

Finally, I dropped to my knees beside a hotel room bed and prayed, God, if you've gone to this much trouble to keep me sober tonight, I will never test you again.

And I haven't. After twenty-five years of sobriety, I still stay out of bars. I have no business in bars. I belong in the meeting rooms of Alcoholics Anonymous with people who know who and what I am.

My Higher Power not only watched over me throughout all those years of drinking, but he is still here today. I try to spend every day of my life practicing awareness of the presence of God.

Bill S.
Roswell, Georgia

Chain of Trust

December 2007

She was very thin and appeared much older than her thirty-five years. She seemed confused, lost. I welcomed her.

She asked me where she should go. I suggested the First Step meeting and guided her to the room. I sat next to her. I asked if she'd like a cup of coffee. She replied, "Only if it has a shot of whiskey in it." I told her I understood, and brought her a plain cup anyway. She could not hold the cup without shaking. She barely sipped it—that was the first time I saw her.

After that, I saw her often at the meetings. She began to share her experience with alcohol.

One night, after a meeting, I gave her my phone number. She called me several times. She talked. We shared. She asked me to be her sponsor.

First Step, Second Step, Third Step, Fourth and Fifth Steps, right through to the Twelfth Step. We read the Big Book together, at least once a week, sometimes twice. We laughed at ourselves. I looked forward to seeing her.

At ten months sober, she picked up a drink, drove into a tree, and died instantly.

I felt the pain of loss. I missed her. I grieved for her. I felt angry at alcohol. I had come to love her and now she was gone.

After many months, the pain eased a bit. I shared my feelings with my sponsor and my friends in AA.

I awoke on a beautiful summer morning and began to think about her and the great gift she had given me. My heart smiled—I was thankful she had come into my life. She had given me the gift of trust. She had indeed been a part of God's gift, insuring my recovery.

I learned we don't love people because they are perfect; if we did, there would be no one to love. Could she know how grateful I am to her?

Three years later, while attending another AA meeting, I saw a young gal walk in with that same look of confusion. I greeted her with a smile, and she said, "This is my first meeting. I'm scared." I assured her that she'd be okay. I offered her coffee and a chair.

After the meeting, she approached me and asked, again, what my name was. I repeated, "Fran."

She said, "You were the one. You knew my mother. She died in a car accident. After being sober for ten months, she picked up a drink and drove. It's been about three years, now. I have a drinking problem. Will you help me?"

My cup runneth over.

Fran H.
L'Anse, Michigan

The Hole in the Soul

May 2005

For thirteen years of my alcoholism, my wife's faith made it possible for her to endure the tornado. Still, she occasionally laments that she has never had the "burning bush" experience some AAs mention. Early on in my alcoholism career, I was a college student foundering about in Prescott, Arizona. While the early signs of booze addiction were popping up all around, it had not yet become the obsession that it later did. And I was a self-proclaimed atheist. As Bill W. put it, I believed that mankind "crawled out of the primordial ooze" and self-determination and propulsion alone were necessary to "get ahead."

The only thing I seemed terribly good at was propelling myself into frustration and depression punctuated by binges with alcohol that brought very temporary relief. Insomnia overshadowed long nights of loneliness and confusion. Ambition and hope collapsed and I began to meticulously plan suicide. End the pain once and for all.

One hot July night I was on my knees wrestling with a stereo that had ceased functioning. It was the straw that broke the camel's back and I began to weep uncontrollably, feeling the depression sweep over me like a cold gray fog. In my anguish, it occurred to me that as I was on my knees, why not just throw a prayer out there into the indifferent universe. Had nothing else to lose.

From my defeat and sorrow I said aloud, "God, I really don't think you exist. In fact, I am probably just wasting my breath right now. But if you do exist, I could really, really use some help right now." In that moment the small, paint-chipped room became illuminated and a wash of peace and serenity came over me. A voice, more like a sound, repeated several times, "Everything will be alright." I don't know how long this episode lasted, but I remained serene and joyful, but also tired for the first time in months.

I crawled onto my mattress and slept soundly and dreamlessly.

The next morning my first conscious thought was, What happened? What was that? Was it an hallucination? Cautiously I crawled onto the floor and slowly arose, almost whiffing the air for the first scent of depression. No, I felt peaceful, rested, serene and optimistic.

This newfound optimism lasted several months. During this time I tried to convey my experience with a few people, but was met with condescension or frank skepticism. Not having any religious training or experience to get my bearings, I really didn't know what to do with this vision, for lack of a better word.

I laid off the booze for a couple of months, but as I began to continue my old efforts at trying to make things work my way, the old depression started to slide in. And I drank. First just a few beers, then a six pack, then up to two six packs. I drank all night, and struggled into classes hungover the following morning.

Two years of feeling the nip of the wringer was about all I could take. Call me a tenderfoot, but the daily cycle of drinking, working, and passing out eroded me to a point of desperation. I went to a therapist and spilled the beans about my solitary and intensive drinking. She said that she probably could not help me with my drinking, as psychotherapy alone was not known to be useful in most alcoholic cases. She suggested I try a meeting of Alcoholics Anonymous.

I did go to a meeting, and seeing those people who described the grip of alcohol, and how they were experiencing a new freedom and new happiness, hit like a lightening bolt. I went home, dumped all my beer down the sink, threw out dozens of empties, and continued to not drink and go to meetings. I got down on my knees and confessed to God that I was powerless over alcohol and that my life was wholly unmanageable. I said as I truly felt, that he could and would relieve me of this obsession to drink and I asked him to do so with complete abandon.

No chariots swinging low and no burning bushes, but I did feel an enormous release—like a weight being lifted off my shoulders. I slept well and my grades picked up. Life was not smooth, but things tended to work out and there were good times and good friends.

After five years of sobriety, I slowly became disenchanted with AA, and a lot of that had to do with not picking up a new sponsor after the Army moved me across the country. I closed down and backed off from AA. Within another year I was drunk, and that slip was to last thirteen horrific years. I lost our house, mangled my marriage, and went in and out of various jobs. Depression hurled down on me worse than I had ever known. It seemed like the booze was the only thing that kept me moving, and I drank as much as I could whenever I could.

After thirteen years, it became clear to me, after a particularly vicious blackout, that I was a hopeless alcoholic. Over the years I just blotted out my AA knowledge with increasing amounts of liquor, until the day came when I could no longer deny that I could not control my drinking and that again my life was a jumbled wreck.

That sunny morning on September 11, 2001 (no relation to the historic date) I dropped to my knees and once again asked God to take over my drinking, that I was powerless to do anything about. I said Steps One, Two, and Three aloud from memory. My skeptical wife, her pretty face drawn with sadness and disappointment, stopped packing her suitcase and said, "All right, one more chance. But I'm not holding my breath."

It took four months of solo-sobriety before I worked up enough nerve, and resentment, to go to an AA meeting. During those four sober months I found an old Grapevine tape and listened to it about twice a day. I found my old Big Book and began to read it very carefully, amazed at how I had shut my eyes to all that was crashing down around me during that thirteen-year slip.

Now I go to meetings regularly, and people know me and I know them. I have a sponsor whom I talk to on a regular basis to check up on my spiritual health What is odd, looking back on it, is that during my active alcoholism I never really feared death, largely because I was simply too drunk to care. My physical health is severely and permanently damaged from the river of alcohol I gladly ingested. What scares me now is not so much having another slip, but turning my back on God. I fear the "hole in the soul."

So where is that manifest presence of the Higher Power we crave? Appendix II in the Big Book (Third Edition) notes that often spiritual awakening is a result of a series of educational experiences, which occur much more often than the "burning bush" phenomenon. A cherished member of our group with many years of recovery, recounted how early in her sobriety she had been to an AA meeting. She had over-imbibed on coffee, drinking some thirty-two cups of the stuff during the day, noting how it resembled her drinking patterns of before. Terry related that she felt horrible and tense and made her way to the back of the clubhouse, where a small foyer housed the restrooms and a soda machine.

Lowering her head to her hand she exclaimed, "God, I really overdid it on coffee today. Just please give me something without caffeine." At that moment the soda machine rumbled and out popped a caffeine-free soda. Terry counts this as her burning bush experience, and it might indicate that God has a heck of a sense of humor.

As for myself, having the burning bush vision definitely laid clear for me that there is a loving God who expresses himself to me. Yet in the day-to-day journey of life it is the experience, strength, and hope of my AA friends that help me stay on track and not pick up that first drink. And when I walk into a meeting of AA, anywhere from Texas to Maine, I see the manifest presence of a Higher Power as expressed in the astonishing reality that almost everyone sitting therein sober by his grace.

Jeff M.
El Paso, Texas

The Hypnotist

April 2004

I used to be a pitiful drunk, sick in body, mind, and spirit. Toward the end of my drinking, I had gin blossoms in my cheeks, neuropathy in my left arm, high blood pressure, and a waxy sheen to my skin. I had frequent panic attacks, and I avoided driving because I couldn't be sure I wouldn't faint. Sometimes, my arms felt as if they were melting off the wheel, and I carried a little paper bag to breath into when the attacks hit.

I decided I'd better do something, so I went to a hypnotist to help me stop smoking. I chose Pauline out of the phone book because her office was the closest to my work. Maybe I didn't read her ad carefully enough, or maybe it just didn't mention that she was a Bible-based hypnotherapist. Had I known, I never would have gone. True, I felt a sad, vague yearning toward faith. But my life was too bleak and damaged to lift up my heart to the possibility of God.

Pauline's office in San Francisco's financial district was in a grand, old, ornate building constructed in the 1920s. The office itself, though, was nondescript and very tiny. I walked in and sat down, and she commenced to explain that she based her hypnosis on the precepts of the Old Testament, particularly the shedding of blood that has represented salvation throughout humankind. I nervously looked around for the door. But I didn't bolt; something made me stay.

She hypnotized me, and I surmise that my brain was distracted for just the split second needed to get a new thought in edgewise.

What she said changed everything. Not since taking my first drink at age sixteen had there been such a complete rearranging of my molecules.

She said, "People who use outside substances are usually seeking a connection with something greater than themselves." Mind you, I hadn't told her about my drinking. I was there on a smoking rap.

One minute I was mired in self-disgust, resigned to drinking myself to death. The next, I was restored to a sense of innocence and innate goodness. Perhaps it was as she said: I was seeking enlightenment but was just sadly, completely, on the wrong path. But I couldn't have formed these thoughts during that hour in her office, even though I remember feeling refreshed as I rode the elevator down to the lobby.

Then something extraordinary happened. There was an exhibit of ethnic dance costumes from around the world encased in clear plexiglass box frames in the lobby, and when I looked at them, the costumes began to shimmer! I could perceive every thread, ribbon, button, and bow. The fabrics pulsed with energy and the colors glowed and radiated auric light. I was mesmerized, but lacked the mental health to recognize a miracle in progress. How I wish I'd stayed a while!

Instead, I bustled away, leaving my cigarettes on top of the nearest trash receptacle for a passerby and heading back to the office. I lasted maybe a day and a half without cigarettes and my drinking continued at its hell-bent pace. But my heart wasn't really in it anymore. I was tired of being so ill. Six months later, I admitted I was powerless over alcohol to my physician at a long-overdue checkup.

"What are we going to do about your drinking?" my doctor asked. "I don't know," I replied. "What are we going to do?" That use of the plural "we" was my First Step. I haven't looked back.

I returned to Pauline to give her faith a go, but I was still not open to the traditional teachings of the major faiths. I aspire to study the Bible one day, but more for its allegorical beauty than its teachings. The spirituality of recovery, specifically AA's Twelve Steps, is just right for me and continues to nourish my body, mind, and soul.

I love the Higher Power I've found in recovery and am awed that I was touched by such a demonstration of life's wonders that day in a San Francisco office building. It gives me even greater incentive for keeping my compass pointed toward spiritual awareness and conscious contact with God. I'm in it for the miracles.

Liz O.
Oakland, California

A Close Shave

July 1985

W
hen I first came to AA (over thirty-eight years ago now), I tried every suggestion in order to kick the bottle. One was to take the Twelve Steps list, cut off each Step, and put the twelve pieces of paper into my shaving kit. (I was a traveling salesman.) Each morning as I reached in for my razor, I'd pull out one of the Steps. This would be the Step I'd concentrate on that day.

Obviously, the original kit was long ago abandoned, along with that little gimmick. But packing for a vacation recently, while getting a couple of practicing alcoholics into the hospital with all the usual confusion and hurry, I somehow threw the old kit into my luggage. By the time I got to the beach, I was pretty tuckered out and was thinking something like this: You're worn out getting these guys to agree to go to the hospital, arranging to see a doctor, getting them to and into the hospital, and trying to take care of their loose ends. You're no spring chicken any longer. Isn't it about time you slowed down on this twelfth-stepping and thought of yourself more?

Ideas like those, based on resentment and self-pity, were running through my mind when I opened the old shaving kit and removed my razor. Stuck to it was a sliver of yellowed paper that read: "Having had a spiritual awakening as the result of these Steps, we tried to carry this message to alcoholics, and to practice these principles in all our affairs."

I didn't see my Higher Power put it there, but neither did I see anyone else. Outside AA, that would be called a coincidence. We in AA call such occurrences miracles and have grown to expect them.

D. T.
Comer, Georgia

When a Sponsee Slips

May 2003

For the last year, I've been sponsoring another alcoholic who's working very hard on his program, harder than he had ever had in the past. It was not his first go at it, but it was his first honest effort. He got a sponsor, started working the Steps, and you could see the miracle starting to happen to him right in front of your eyes. Then, after marking his first year of sobriety, he started to get complacent. He went to fewer and fewer meetings, his phone calls got fewer and farther apart, and when he did call, I could hear a certain dissatisfaction with life starting to creep into his voice. Within weeks, he went out again, and although he has been showing up at meetings to get twenty-four hour chips every few days, he has not been able to make it back yet. Everyone is wondering how he is doing.

His slide happened so quickly after he slacked off, it proved to me how much a twenty-four-hour program this is. Intellectually, I knew his future was in God's hands, but inside I wanted so much to help him that I called and chased him for a some time. My sponsor suggested that maybe it was time I cut him loose and let him go before I got dragged down with him. I usually try to listen to my sponsor, but on this point I couldn't agree with him. I loved my friend and didn't want to be yet another person giving up hope on him because he had slipped. Yet, soon his slide began affecting my life more than I realized. It was all I thought about at work, at home, and even when I should have been sleeping.

My sponsor finally got through to me, saying "You know, you can do this for as long as you want, and I'll never tell you when to stop. But you have got to realize sooner or later how powerless you are over this." I'm not really sure why those words finally hit me. I guess it's like my last drink: I'm not really sure why it happened when it did, but it happened, and today I accept that.

So this evening, when I spoke to my friend, I finally told him in no uncertain terms that he had to finish what he'd started, that I cared about him, and that he needed to try to find someone he was willing to work with when, or if, he comes back. And then I told him that I had to let him go. When I hung up the phone, I started to cry. I don't really think I expected that to happen. My fiance looked at me and said, "Call your sponsor." So I did.

My sponsor simply said, "You'll be okay. Go to a meeting and find a newcomer to work with."

As I was getting ready to follow his suggestion and leave for a meeting (about fifteen minutes after talking with my sponsee), the phone rang. It was our local AA hotline calling to ask if I would take a call from a guy who needed help. I wrote down the number, called the person, and within half an hour, I'd picked him up and was getting him a cup of coffee at a meeting. We have a plan to meet for tomorrow night, too.

Sometimes God doesn't ask me to read between the lines. I believe that as long as I keep doing the things Alcoholics Anonymous suggests, I won't drink today. And maybe, just maybe, I might be able to help another alcoholic in the process.

Dave R.
Manchester, New Hampshire

A Lost Son's Blessing

October 2008

During my drinking, I was married twice and had six children. My first husband was an alcoholic who abandoned me and our four young children. I subsequently married again and gave birth to two more sons, whom I abandoned in my drunkenness, leaving them to be raised by their abusive father. Although I did not become aware of certain facts until my own recovery began, I knew my first husband had found AA and my youngest daughter, Susan, had found Al-Anon. Susan had always loved and cared for her two younger half-brothers and actually raised Eric, the older of the two, through his teens.

In April 1991, Eric came back to live with me, though just a few months later, he was killed in a car accident, while making a run to the "Beer Barn." Eric was only twenty-one years old at the time.

I was still drinking back then and, although I was certainly in a state of shock, I have vivid memories of that night. I remember following the ambulance to the hospital, viewing his body and signing the papers to donate his organs. I remember that I was very uncomfortable with the concept of religion or God, so when I was asked at the hospital if I wanted a priest to say a few words for Eric, I adamantly rejected the idea. I remember saying I wanted nothing to do with anything religious.

Each year, as the anniversary of Eric's death drew closer, I would experience tremendous fear and anxiety. My preferred method of handling that terrible fear was to take the day off from work, get high, get drunk, and finish up with a new tattoo to memorialize the day. Basically, I would just stay drunk.

In August 1997, I came into AA and had just eighty-eight days of sobriety when the anniversary of Eric's death came around again. I started sharing at meetings about how frightening this date was for me and how I did not want to drink over it. Using the program and all its tools, I was able to push through the fear and, instead of drinking, I went out and got a special tattoo, something to commemorate my love for my son. I stayed close to the rooms, my sponsor, and my AA friends, and I did not pick up a drink.

The night of the anniversary, at 10:55, the exact time of Eric's death, I dropped to my knees and starting crying. It was then that I found myself praying to a God that I could now feel was there for me. I found a loving God that night and he has never left me since.

Two days later, I'd completed my first ninety days of sobriety. My youngest son, Rick, had just moved in temporarily with me. He promised no drinking or drugging in my house and was obeying this rule. On this particular morning, I woke up and was having my coffee when Rick came downstairs, so I shared with him that I was sober ninety days that very day. He asked me to wait a minute, ran back upstairs, and came down again, saying he had something for me. He had a plastic zip-top bag with the words "Frankford/Torresdale Hospital" on it. That was the hospital where Eric died.

Rick unzipped the bag and took out Eric's wallet, necklace, hash pipe, roach clip, and lighter. I was shocked, as I had not realized he had possession of Eric's final belongings. He said he had been carrying this bag with him for all the years since Eric died.

Then Rick told me there was one more thing, and he pulled out an AA coin, saying that the coin had meant a lot to Eric because he'd carried it every day and switched it from pocket to pocket. Eric had told Rick his sponsor had given him the coin. I looked at the coin and it was a medallion for ninety days. Apparently Eric had come into the program, but had not stayed. I never did learn how long Eric had remained sober.

I had not known about his attempt at recovery at the time and later learned that his sponsor had been none other than my first husband (now deceased), who had preceded me into recovery years ago. Eric had received the coin in 1985 and had carried it until his death in 1991. Now I carry the coin with love and gratitude, for all that it stood for in his life and now stands for in mine. I turn my will and my life over to the care of God every morning and thank him every night. And I have not had to pick up a drink, one day at a time, for ten years.

Nanci R.
Floral City, Florida

No Accident

January 2010

I was 18 years old and scraping along, just above bottom. I had all kinds of problems. I had no money, my truck had blown its motor and I had ongoing relationship issues with everyone around me. I was irritable, discontent and angry at life. I had quit school the year before and was living in a small house with a couple of other guys my age. I was drinking and using any mood-altering substance I could find. I barely managed to keep a job working for my brother, although he didn't want people to know we were related.

Two friends came over to help me put the motor in my truck. As usual, this type of work consisted mostly of drinking beer. Once we had the motor in and running, we hit the liquor store, bought three cases of beer and went to a party I'd heard about near the beach. The events of that night are hazy. I remember leaving the party. Two girls were in the front seat with me; my friends got relegated to the back of the truck and were sitting on a wooden box that I kept tools in. I was thinking that I probably shouldn't be driving; however, that didn't stop me. We made it back into town, and as I went to turn a corner, what happened next changed my life.

Both of my friends fell out of my truck, one out of the driver's side and one out of the passenger side. I stopped the truck. My friends were lying on the ground, not moving. There was blood and broken glass. Someone called the police and I heard sirens. I ran to the truck, got the booze and drugs and hid them in the bushes nearby. I was already saying the alcoholic prayer: "God get me outta this one; I will never do it again."

The police and the ambulances came; my friends were taken to the hospital and the police interviewed me. I admitted that I had been drinking, but I said that it had been hours before. I acted like I was trying to help a few drunken friends get home. I was a hero, helping people out. The cops bought it. I went to the hospital for a while and then was told to go home.

Once I got home I couldn't sleep. I relived the events of the night over and over again. Around 7 A.M. I got a phone call from one of my injured friends, asking for a ride home from the hospital. I picked him up. Luckily he was not seriously hurt; he just had a few scrapes and a minor concussion. My other friend had been released about an hour earlier and he also had minor injuries. About two hours later, I still couldn't sleep, so I decided to get some gas. On the way home,

I rear-ended a car at a speed of around 50 kph. The two people in the car were luckily wearing their seatbelts. They both had injuries but nothing that required hospitalization. Their car, however, was a write-off.

The police again attended, and again I blamed others for what had happened. I wouldn't have hit that car if it wasn't stopped in my lane, if the other lane wasn't blocked by an RV, etc. I had an excuse for everything. The police issued me a ticket for speeding and told me to go home. I could still drive my truck. I went to my parents' house and told them about rear-ending the car, but not about the accident where my friends flew out of my truck. They bought into my blaming and became just as righteously indignant as I was.

Later on that day, all I could do was reflect on how screwed up my life had gotten. I could have killed four people in less than 12 hours in two separate accidents. I couldn't believe my luck. If it weren't for bad luck I'd have no luck at all. I felt as low as I thought I could get. (I found out later I could get lower.) I wanted to die, I hurt so bad. I couldn't remember a time when I didn't hurt. I knew deep down that the alcohol and the other substances were killing me, but I couldn't see living without them.

I thought of my older brother. He went to AA and I had seen the change in him. He had gone from a hopeless alcoholic to a sober, fun-loving guy—the brother I'd admired as a child. Whatever had happened to Sam clearly was a miracle. I thought maybe he had something. He had hinted a few times that the program would benefit me, and he'd told me about the way his life had changed. He tried to explain unmanageability and powerlessness; he tried to explain serenity and peace. He had suggested I come and see what it was all about, but he never pushed.

I quickly decided that it wasn't a good idea to phone my brother. Chances were I would quit anyway; I never really stuck with anything. I called AA and spoke to a woman who said she would have a member phone me back. A few minutes later the phone rang and a man asked me if I had inquired about AA. He asked if I had had a drink that day, then suggested we get together for a coffee and then possibly attend a meeting. I agreed to meet him at a local restaurant.

By the time I got there, I had somehow convinced myself that things weren't so bad, that I was probably overreacting. I felt like the victim of a cosmic conspiracy. I just about had myself convinced to turn around when the man introduced himself. We sat down and he told me about his drinking; he told me about some of his more unmanageable moments. I remember thinking, It's a good thing this guy doesn't drink anymore. I was busy looking for the differences, not the similarities.

Toward the end of our coffee, he paused, looked at me, and said something that still amazes me. "You know you're about the same age as my son." I didn't say anything, and he continued, "I wish he would do something about his drinking." I asked him why and he replied, "Last night he was drinking, and he fell out of some guy's truck and nearly died." I was amazed! Being a consummate actor, I didn't allow him to know what I was feeling inside. We went to the meeting, and I was still numb from his story about his son. It was only a surprise to me when I relapsed in spectacular fashion two weeks later.

Three years and a lot of unnecessary pain and wreckage later, I celebrated my first year with a cake. I had moved far away, but I was planning on being in Vancouver. I had something to say to that man, if I found him. When I got there I asked around at meetings, and someone who knew him told me where his home group was. I got there just as it ended, saw Bill and went up to him. He recognized me and we shook hands. I told him that I had just taken a one-year cake and had something to say to him. He interrupted me and said, "Before you say anything, there's someone I want you to meet." He led me into the back room and we approached a guy at the sink washing dishes. He said, "I think you guys know each other." It was his son, one of the guys who had fallen out of my truck that night three years before. We hugged and laughed. I asked Bill how he knew. He said that when he told me the story about his son, my eyes had gotten as big as saucers. We laughed again. All that time, I thought that I'd hidden it so well.

Even before I found a loving Higher Power in this program, I knew that my friend's dad twelfth-stepping me was no coincidence. Of all the AA people in a town the size of Vancouver, the one who called was the father of the guy I almost killed the night before. It was, and still is, mind-boggling.

Mike T.
Prince George, British Columbia

EXCERPTED FROM
Highland Sobriety

May 2005

For eighteen months, I tried on my own to stay sober, but I could not. Sometimes I lasted a week or a fortnight, but eventually I would take that first drink and that was it, another night on the booze and another morning of regrets. The end of this eighteen months self-imposed solitary struggle culminated in another holiday. This time I was in Jersey, in the Channel Islands.

After three days, I went to a folk club. As usual the folk club was held in a bar and when I went in, I wasn't sure whether I was going to have a pint of coke or a pint of stout. Fortunately I asked for the cola and had a very enjoyable evening. The next day I felt very agitated and as I walked around St. Helier, I started to feel very thirsty. I knew I wanted a drink. I didn't know what to do. Just then I looked in a gift shop window and I saw the Serenity Prayer engraved on a glass dish. I had only ever seen or heard the Serenity Prayer at the AA meeting. I knew that I had to get in touch with AA right away.

I went to a phone box intending to get the AA phone number from directory inquiries. Inside the phone box however, someone had put a card with the AA number on it. I phoned straight away and within five minutes I was at a meeting which just "happened" to be starting in a church hall yards from the phone box I was using.

That day I believe I had a spiritual awakening and that my Higher Power led me back to AA. For that and the contentment I have been given, I am very thankful.

Jim B.
Glasgow, Scotland

The Peter Principle

April 1996

In 1969, when I was sixteen years old, I had a baby boy whom I named Peter. I saw him once, immediately after he was born, and then I gave him to a social worker and he was placed with his new family. With this he passed from my life completely. This event, which to most people would have been an agonizing affair, affected me on the surface very little. But the "Twelve and Twelve" tells us that damaging emotional conflicts which persist below the level of consciousness may give our emotions violent twists which will alter our lives for the worse. This appears to have been true with me as I went blithely on with my life, never discussing what I had done or even thinking much about it. In fact, I told people that the baby had died and later I denied ever having had a child. However, my drug and alcohol intake increased rapidly. By nineteen, I was living on the streets and in the throes of alcoholism that was beyond belief. I stayed drunk continuously (unless I was in jail, psychiatric hospitals, or mental institutions) until I was twenty-nine years old. Then, faced with a physical problem that made it impossible for me to force a drink down my throat, I entered AA in Dallas.

I've stayed active in the Fellowship since then. I have worked the Steps, been sponsored, done service work, and sponsored others. When doing Step Nine, I contacted the adoption registry board where Peter had been placed for adoption. I made myself available so that should he ever wish to contact me, he could do so.

I would not intrude in his life because I believed that was not my right and I felt it could possibly harm him. In working with my sponsor I readily acknowledged that I had a son but truly I felt that his absence in my life didn't affect me.

In August 1995, I received a phone call from my father saying that Peter was looking for me, and at eight that night I called Canada and heard my son's voice for the first time. In the space of five minutes, all the pieces of my life fell into place. He asked when we could meet and I told him that, unbelievably, I was leaving in twelve hours for a planned vacation in Canada, a short distance from where he lived. Had the call come the next day I would have already left for a cottage with no telephone, and wouldn't have heard of his search for me until I had returned to Alabama.

The following Thursday, I walked into the lobby of a hotel and immediately picked my twenty-five-year-old, six-foot-three-inch, 225-pound baby boy out of the crowd. We spent three days together. He is a happy, healthy, well-adjusted young man who has had an "ideal childhood" (his words). The Promises came true for me when we were talking down by the river. He was telling me of his likes and dislikes, his successes and the people in his life. After a pause, he said he would like to tell me some things that he had never told anyone else. I said that would be all right and I listened to the recital of his few sins. Silence followed. Then the whole program of Alcoholics Anonymous fell into place for me when I was able to say that I, too, had done things like that. I told him that there were a few things that had worked for me, and I told him about AA.

Two days later I boarded the plane to return to the States, with a bouquet of flowers in my hand from my son who had thanked me for the decision I made twenty-five years ago. I was so very grateful to AA: That the woman my son had found was healthy, happy, and sober, instead of a prison inmate in Texas, a patient in a psychiatric hospital in Nevada, a drunk in Las Vegas, or merely the record of a suicide in California—any of which could have been my fate if I had continued drinking. We hope to develop a relationship now and I am willing to be of help to him in any way I can. I thank God for this opportunity.

Anna A.
Gulf Shores, Alabama

My Heavenly Fit

January 2002

The most important thing that has happened to me in the last year is the realization that I am an alcoholic. It probably wasn't hard for anyone else to recognize, but I was the last to know. It took over twenty years of hard drinking for me to reach my bottom. On any given day I would drink all the liquor available or pass out, whichever came first. I was thirty pounds overweight, had an impatient, egocentric attitude, and a bloated, ruddy face. Peppermint schnapps was my constant companion. It didn't smell too bad, could pass for mouthwash in a pinch, and, best of all, I could drink it straight, so a mixer wasn't necessary. The bottle rested in a little nook under the front seat of my truck, always at the ready.

The only thing that Amy, my significant other, asked for her birthday last year was that I not drink any alcohol for her birthday weekend. It wasn't an unreasonable request and reflects the desperation she felt about our relationship. She had stood by me in some of the most shameless and embarrassing moments of my life. Nevertheless, just when Amy needed me most, I proceeded to get totally blitzed as I had so many times before. I didn't even bother to get her a birthday gift.

The moment of truth came when the sex and drugs and alcohol were gone. It was that soulful instant of utter despair when no matter how hard I tried, I couldn't get drunk enough. I had just finished chugging the last of a case of wine around 4:00 A.M. when I found myself wandering in the backyard dazed, lonely, and afraid, full of self-pity, guilt, and shame. In my despair, I looked up at the sky and found a power greater than myself.

Before me, a silver sliver of moon hung above the western horizon. It was brilliant enough to be clearly seen, but not so overpowering as to diminish the stars which dazzled and twinkled by the thousands. From the center of the lunar sickle, three planets extended in a line so true that a master craftsman could not have plumbed it straighter. Mars, Venus, and Jupiter danced in the early morning sky.

I am not going to tell you that three planets and the moon have never been aligned like that before. But I have looked up into the sky searching for guidance and direction numerous times and the only response was emptiness. Never before had anything seemed to fit so perfectly together. It was at that moment that

I realized that I too fit into this world, that I too fit into this universe. With all the laws and forces necessary to keep those planets and stars in line, there was a place for me and it was right here and right now. In a flash, I realized that I was a part of this wonderful balance of life.

I had always felt cut off from any sense of spiritual experience. But in allowing myself to be a part of the world instead of fighting it, I found my humanity. Whether there actually is a God is anybody's guess. In the final analysis, though, it really doesn't matter what I believe in as long as I have a sincere belief in a Higher Power. Allowing myself to believe in God, I could allow myself to be human. It was a start, and something I could really sink my teeth into.

My first Higher Power was the universe, and to this day whenever I need strength I just step outside and look for a celestial body like the sun or a star. This allows me to experience again that wonderful feeling of union with my creator. The sensation of fitting in for someone who has always felt like an outsider is an exquisitely rare feeling. It is what I call my Heavenly Fit.

Rick F.
Salt Lake City, Utah

SECTION FOUR

AA's Big Hoop

"At this juncture, his AA sponsor usually laughs. This, the newcomer
thinks, is just about the last straw. This is the beginning of the end. And
so it is: the beginning of the end of his old life, and the beginning of his
emergence into a new one. His sponsor probably says, 'Take it easy. The
hoop you have to jump through is a lot wider than you think.'"

Step Two: *Twelve Steps and Twelve Traditions*

A n editor of AA Grapevine once cited a classic story told by spiritual
teachers, having to do with the pilgrim who comes to a spiritual master
in search of God. The seeker points out that he has given up all things—
wealth, friends, family, possessions—in his quest for a God who has so
far eluded him. He asks the master what else he must do to find God.

What he is told by the master is that he must give up one more thing: his
idea of God.

Nothing is more inspiring than bearing witness to someone's vision of the
light when he or she had been sure—so utterly certain—there was nothing but
darkness. We see that happen every day in the rooms of Alcoholics Anonymous,
where we are daily reminded that we have reached the twenty-first century, and
are holding hands at the end of our meetings with struggling people, many of
whom in no way share the religious beliefs of our co-founders.

If our big hoop is to be more than empty words, these members, who fully
share our desire to stop drinking, must also be able to share our program, fully
and without reservation.

Whether praying to the Great Spirit of the sweat lodge, placing a hopeless life
into the hands of a group, clinging to the universal spirit of humanity, or marveling
at stars dancing in a night sky, our diverse, creative, searching members have found
the spiritual awakening they need in order to claim the priceless gift of sobriety.

These are some of their enlightening stories.

The Hoop Gets Bigger

June 2010

I n 1987, I had told the head of the psychiatric ward at the naval hospital that they needed to get my boss help. I had made the mistake of telling them that I had briefly considered suicide in response to the pressures from my boss. They took away all my clothes, gave me a furry blue robe and a pair of one-size-fits-none slippers. After a week of interviews and testing, they told me I was depressed because I had been drinking large amounts of a depressant—alcohol. They explained that recovery from depression was slow and unremarkable, sometimes taking many years; but if I was possibly an alcoholic, recovery from depression would be rapid and easy. I told them that I thought I might be an alcoholic, because secretly I was looking for the easier, softer way. They asked me if I would like to go to a meeting of Alcoholics Anonymous next door in the Alcohol Rehabilitation Center (ARC). I gave them some feeble excuse why I could not go (like I had something better do while locked up in the mental ward?). The doctor looked at the nurse and said, "Denial." A week later, they transferred me to the ARC and forced me to go to an AA meeting.

I walked into the meeting room as nervous as an atheist at a gathering of holy rollers. The room was furnished with two brown, simulated-wood-grain tables, pushed together in the center of the room, surrounded by brown folding chairs. Around the outer walls were orange wire chairs with foam cushions.

On the center tables near the north wall, were pamphlets with titles like, "Are You an Alcoholic?" and "A Members View of AA," a basket and a blue book entitled Alcoholics Anonymous. The walls were decorated with cheap frames that held black and red calligraphy that said, "Easy Does It," "First Things First," "One Day At A Time" and "Think, Think, Think." On the wall at the head of the table were two window shades with The Twelve Steps and The Twelve Traditions printed on them.

I hid in the south corner of the room, sitting as far away as possible from those pamphlets, afraid that someone might ask me to talk. Shortly, more people arrived, laughing and joking, with big smiles. These people sat near the north end of the room. They were followed by others who looked remarkably like me—hopeless and lost. These people joined me in the back of the room. We shared the look of a person who knows that if he does not stop drinking, it will kill him, yet his body tells him he will die if he does stop drinking; a seemingly hopeless state of mind and body.

The people with smiles read the Preamble, "How It Works," The Twelve Steps and The Twelve Traditions. I heard them use the "G" word (God) a couple of times, and wondered what kind of religious cult they were forcing on me. Would I be brainwashed? The more they talked, the more I could identify with what alcoholism had done to me. I was beginning to learn that alcoholism was a disease—like an allergy; just one drink would trigger the allergy, and at some point I would lose control and not be able to stop when I wanted to. That point would progressively draw nearer and nearer.

The solution was not to have that first drink. God, that was simple! Why didn't I think of that? But I had used alcohol for so long to escape from the realities and pain of life, I did not know how to deal with life's problems or joys without it.

As people continued to share, I began to feel hope, as if I'd been drowning and had been thrown a life preserver. Here they were in front of me, examples of recovery, full of joy and love. They had learned how to be happy in life without alcohol. Maybe I could be happy again. Maybe life could be worth living after all.

Then my life preserver lost its air. They relied on a "Higher Power." I felt as if I had seen heaven and then been told I could not go there. I left that meeting devastated, knowing all was lost. I did not have faith in God and I did not know how to pray. I thought I was doomed to an alcoholic death.

Fortunately, I was not allowed to crawl back into the bottle. They sent me back out to more meetings. I continued to learn that the hoop I needed to jump through for recovery was getting bigger and bigger.

My first prayers were, "Please help" upon waking, and, "Thanks" when going to bed. I was afraid that God, when I found him, would abandon me and I would drink again. I learned that it was my "God as I understood him," that I could have any concept of God I wanted and that the program of recovery would still work. I decided that he could not abandon me, and I have not had that fear of drinking since that time. The turning point in my recovery happened while I driving. It was a beautiful summer day and the temperature was around 70 degrees. I had the sunroof open and was powering through the corners with ease. The car was purring smoothly. The trees were in their summer's finest. I was listening to a tape that explained that faith in a Higher Power is not required to recover from alcoholism; only the belief and reliance on a Higher Power.

The Second Step in Alcoholics Anonymous is, "Came to believe that a Power greater than ourselves could restore us to sanity." I then had faith that my Higher Power (whom I choose to call God) could and would relieve my alcoholism.

I understood how the program worked and knew that I would recover.

The car then filled with a beautiful light. A warm feeling spread throughout my body, and tears of joy cascaded down my cheeks. I felt at peace with the world and one with my God.

Patrick H.

Bellevue, Washington

Prayer

January 1980

T he AA program only suggests that newcomers attempt to begin to conceive of a power greater than themselves, in their own individual terms. After that, an old-timer might suggest to a skeptical newcomer—along with not picking up the first drink—faking prayer and keeping an open mind.

I came into this program a drunken atheist. Today, I pray. My being sober is a reflection of the good attributes of some higher power; it is not a reflection of any moral virtue or strength of will on my part.

This change in a drunken, hard-core, cynical atheist is a miracle beyond human comprehension. However, one aspect of the program has always been required for me to remain sober—results. Prayer works. If prayer didn't work and show results, I'd become an atheist again today.

Spirituality happens to be extremely practical. Prayer, reading the AA literature, going to meetings, using the Steps, and helping another alcoholic all combine to make my life easier and more comfortable, hour to hour, day to day.

As an atheist, I faked prayer on a trial basis in the beginning. The results have altered my viewpoint of the cosmos. An unseen realm does exist. I do not attend church, nor have I experienced a spiritual awakening; I'm still a fire-breathing cynic. Yet I pray regularly to something unseen and so vast that I, as a human being, can never understand or even name it.

I pray because of the positive results that flow from prayer. I'm a pragmatist. So, for today, I have become an agnostic, who occasionally experiences violent swings toward faith. With all the blessings that have been bestowed upon me in a year and a half, I still experience doubts and have not made that quantum leap to faith.

All this proves only one thing: that some nuts are tougher to crack than others. Today, I'm still faking prayer and getting results. Maybe God likes nuts, especially the hard ones.

R. E.

Philadelphia, Pennsylvania

Who I Was and Who I Am Now

October 2008

I was born in 1946, in the small town of Homestead, outside Pittsburgh, Pennsylvania, and was named Richard. Everyone knew me and my parents well, and it was here that I started my journey of three lives: the first as an alcoholic, not yet fully developed; the second as the male whom society accepted, if I behaved myself; and the third as the female inside me, whom many people to this day condemn. You see, I am a transgendered male to female.

In my childhood, my parents drank. My mother would have a drink now and then, and my father was an alcoholic, in my opinion. As an only child, I tried to live up to everyone's expectations. I would say to myself that I'd never get as bad as my father. When I was nine years old, my parents went their separate ways because of my father's drinking. In my teen years, I would hang out with older males and nip a drink now and then. It helped me forget my secrets and my desire to fit in.

I couldn't talk to anyone because I feared their misunderstanding of who and what I really was. I didn't drink in bars (all the bar owners knew me and my family) until age twenty-one. I started drinking more on weeknights and weekends. I joined clubs to feel safe, and hide who I was. I also joined the army to be the man everyone wanted me to be, and that didn't work out. I still drank when I could. I tried getting married, had two children, and drank after work. I ended up going to detox centers and rehabs many times, in order to save my job and my marriage of nine years, but it didn't work out for me.

By now I was sleeping in rooming houses on top of bars and drinking more. I had fear and loneliness inside. At the age of thirty-five, I ran away to join the circus, to hide my secret life. I thought that now I could be the king of the road, only to become a bum with a buck. You see, when I climbed on that circus train, I took something with me—myself. That's the hardest thing to get away from.

I don't know when or where I crossed the line into alcoholism. I tried to stop. I was in and out of AA and hospital detoxes. I lived in a halfway house, and had a psychiatric hospital stay because I tried to kill myself by jumping out a window, and failed. I was drinking again and not knowing who or what I was.

Seven years ago, I detoxed by myself. It's not a good thing to do, and I wouldn't wish that on anyone.

I went back to AA and got a sponsor. I also had to get the acceptance that was the key to solving all my problems. I had to admit that I was powerless over alcohol and that my life was unmanageable. I needed a manager because I couldn't manage my life. I needed a Higher Power, a God of my understanding. I knew about God, but turned to him only in desperation.

Step Three told me I had to make a decision to turn my will and life over to the God of my understanding. I still don't know if God is a he, she, or it, and to me it doesn't matter. What matters is I came to believe in a Higher Power, whom I call God, and I have a sponsor to help me with the Steps.

Things today are not all ice cream and cake, but it is a new life. With my Higher Power and sponsor walking with me, I've been able to change my name. My legal name is now Ricki, and I live my life as a female. I've been sober seven years, and I'm sixty-two years old. I know that I am still one drink away from the unknown, but for my Higher Power, my sponsor, and the many people in AA who have faith in me. My name is Ricki and I am an alcoholic, first and last.

Ricki P.
Homestead, Pennsylvania

The Uncertainty Principle

September 1995

If I don't believe in a God, what is my Higher Power? How can I apply the Steps? What is it that helps me, an agnostic, get sober and stay sober? I gave up searching for an understanding of my Higher Power. Call it a character defect if you will, but I simply cannot believe. So how do I apply the principles of AA? How do I stay sober?

Strange as it may seem, I am helped mostly by Steps Three and Seven. I turn my will and my life and all things over to the care of anything but me. Instead of going against the stream of life, running my head against walls, trying to do the impossible, I turn the outcome of my endeavors to the natural flow of things. I constantly remind myself that I cannot control my fellow humans. Their lives are controlled by the laws of nature, just as mine are. I remind myself, whatever I do, that I never have all the facts affecting the outcome. I do the best I can with the data available, but I can't plan on the outcome. In physics there is something called an "uncertainty principle." Chance and the unknown play too much a part in my daily life to insist on a certain outcome.

But this "turning over" is essentially an act of nonaction. Nonaction in the past was my downfall; it led to my concentrating on myself and my problems. So what else must I do? The key here lies in the recognition that the worst problem for an alcoholic is self-centeredness. The solution to that problem is concentration on others. What keeps me sober and serene is the very act of letting go of resentments, self-pity, fear of others, and whatever else keeps my thoughts going in circles about myself. While I'm occupied with paying attention to the needs of others, I'm free of myself. I don't mean to imply that I shouldn't take care of myself. My natural needs must be met. But no more is required.

Step Seven, which asks the Higher Power to relieve me from all defects that stand in the way of my usefulness to my fellows, is the active complement of Step Three. In the Seventh Step prayer I see that the believer simply asks to be a good person. A "good person" is a person who does no harm to others, a person who helps others. As long as I'm a good person, I need not fear others. As long as I take care to know what acts of mine might harm others, I'm not concentrated on myself, but on others. I stay sober. In Steps Four, Five, and Six, I've learned what defects of mine tend to hurt others. Constant vigilance against these defects keeps me on my toes, keeps me away from getting stuck in the rut of self-pity, fear, and resentment. I practice the opposite of the defect. Instead of letting fear of failure lead me into procrastination, I practice doing difficult things first. Instead of letting impatience bring my brain to a boil, I practice patience. It's easy to fall back into bad habits. By practicing the opposite, I practice and acquire good habits. Still, I need Step Ten to avoid falling back, and meditation in Step Eleven to learn more of what is required of me to stay happy and serene without a drink.

My Higher Power? The laws of nature—those I know of, and those I don't know of.

Oktavia C.
Galveston, Texas

How I Took Step Two

November 2002

I had been in the program about a month and a half when my sponsor and I had "one of those talks."

"You have to believe in God," he said.

"There is no God," said I. I had not believed in God since I was in fifth or sixth grade. In the intervening thirty years, I had built a formidable intellectual edifice against God. There was no God, and I could prove it. Naturally, I was having a hard time with Step Two.

It's not that I hadn't been trying. I had gone around to several people I respected, in search of an atheistic spirituality. I believed there were powers greater than I: get hit by a bus, I thought, and you'll find a power greater than yourself. I attended Quad A meetings—Alcoholics Anonymous for Atheists and Agnostics. They talked about the group being a power greater than self. I had also heard "Good Orderly Direction." I knew the litany. Nothing grabbed me. I was a scientist, and scientifically there was a lot of evidence that there is no supernatural, no inexplicable force doing things in the world. Man had created God in his own image and imbued Him with his peculiarly human powers of creativity.

We continued this discussion for what seemed like five minutes. In short, it was pretty inane. I finally said, in exasperation, "Maybe I'm in the wrong program."

"No! You're in the right program!" was the sharp reply.

I was contemplating this, sitting on the back porch smoking a cigarette. I had tried to quit, but been unsuccessful. My treatment program had told me, "First Things First. One thing at a time. You can quit smoking later." My wife didn't want me smoking inside, so I was on the back porch in January contemplating what I was going to do with the program. His final statement had been common ground. I was in the right program. Besides, I had nowhere else to turn.

"I'm right and he's wrong. There is no God," I thought. I mulled this over and over in my head. "He's wrong and yet he has the program. In order to get it, I have to have a higher power, but I'm right, there is no God."

It was then that the moment of clarity came. I have since heard that a spiritual awakening is easy: any time any alcoholic anywhere understands any part of the truth, that's a spiritual awakening. It occurred to me that what was important to me was that I was right and my sponsor was wrong. I knew. I was scientific and tried to follow the dictates of science. But by then I had heard, and believed, that my best thinking had got me here. I knew, beyond any shadow of a doubt, that I had not the slightest idea how to live my life. I had been an utter failure, and that's how I got to AA.

I thought, I can give that up. I realized I didn't have to be right. More than that, I thought, You know, maybe I ought to believe just because they tell me to. It would help me remember that I don't know everything. It would be inconsistent and all my thinking has had to be so damn consistent that I wound up in AA. I once heard that "foolish consistency is the hobgoblin of little minds." Maybe I needed to be a little bigger and be able to say, "Yeah, I admit I don't know everything. I'm so blasted scientific, yet I believe in God." I felt a real calm. I went about my business.

Later that afternoon I went to my Quad A meeting. I commented on my little epiphany. During the meeting, I realized that I was smoking a cigarette but I didn't want it. I left the pack on the table. I have not had a desire to smoke a cigarette, or, for that matter, take a drink of alcohol, since that date, more than a dozen years ago.

I have always thought that was the narrowest possible basis on which to base a belief in God. But through even that little crack of the door, the light shone through. My faith in God has grown immeasurably. I pray on my knees each morning and evening and in less formal ways throughout the day. I see today that God was doing for me what I could not do for myself. It was God that brought me to AA and to my sponsor. And it was AA that brought me to God.

Bruce P.
Chicago, Illinois

One Hundred Years and Counting

December 2004

Today, on my one hundredth birthday, my "babies" are taking me out to lunch to celebrate. I've sponsored dozens of women in the past fifty-three years of my sobriety, and now most of my babies are twenty and thirty years sober. I haven't sponsored anyone new in the past ten years because my hearing is almost gone. But I learned so much from my babies. They would ask a difficult question, and I had to go to my Big Book to find the answer. I've read that book hundreds of times.

I still go to meetings once a week, especially at the ABC Club of Indio, California. I can't hear a thing anyone says, but I know what is going on. Everyone is talking about a problem with their job, their relationship, or their family. It is important for me to be there, as I receive lots of hugs and kisses.

Also, I just love alcoholics. I love every one of them. I may not like what they do, but I love them. I give them the right to be who they are and do whatever they do and that frees me from resentments.

I am so grateful. I accept the things I cannot change. And growing older presents a lot of things I cannot change—and so a lot of acceptance.

The only thing I can change is my attitude. And my attitude is one of such gratitude. I have a wonderful family, had two wonderful husbands, good health, and a great relationship with my Higher Power—now. But I had a terrible time getting a relationship with God. It took about five years and I couldn't say "God" during that time. I always said "HP." But then something clicked and we've been strong since then.

Albertine R.
Yucca Valley, California

How I Found Alcoholics Anonymous In Perambur

December 2002

After many years of glorious drinking and sometimes glorious oblivion, then after many years of being sick and tired of being sick and tired, even after promising God, myself, and others that my next drink would be my last, I decided to give religion a try. I decided to go for confession. I picked the youngest priest in the parish. Poor chap, he was stunned when I told him that it had been twenty-seven years since my last confession. He must have been two or three years older than my eldest son, who was twenty-seven plus. I was fifty-two years old, and this was in June 1988.

The place: Perambur, India.

It was hardly a confession. I kept harping on my excessive drinking. It was a face-to-face confession. No anonymous confessional box. "Uncle," the young priest said to me, "coming to church, praying, and crying will not help you. You have to go to Alcoholics Anonymous. You have to talk to another person with the same problem you have." I couldn't believe this advice was coming from a priest.

So off I went to 17 Balfour Road, at Kelly's Corner, as suggested by the priest. The moment I entered the gates, I became almost petrified. There, on the walls, I saw slogans and other writings which disturbed me. "Good Lord," I thought, "this is a Protestant set-up. Why did that priest send me here?" Suddenly, it seemed, I had became a very devout Catholic.

When I entered the AA meeting room, I found a bunch of nice, intelligent-looking chaps—all younger than I. I don't recall what was actually said, but I do know that they were talking about booze. When I walked into that AA room, I had, what I later learned is known in AA as a wet brain. (It still feels damp at times.)

After the meeting, I walked up to the first chap who smiled at me, shook his hand, and said "My name is Ronny H. I'm a Roman Catholic!" The man looked at me, his face lit up with a broad smile, and he said, "My name is Jallal. I'm a Muslim." Lord, Lord! What is this? I thought to myself. Why has this priest sent me here? I expected to meet a Matthew, Mark, Luke, or John, or some Tom, Dick, or Harry. This was something else!

This was how I found that wonderful Fellowship of Alcoholics Anonymous. I did drink again. I went on a couple of binges in August 1988, but that's another story. But after every binge, I went to an AA meeting and spoke about it. No one questioned how it had happened or why it had happened. All I heard was "Keep coming. It works."

AA has worked for me one day at a time since September 1, 1988. All this could not have happened if not for that Benevolent Force that most of us call God.

Ronny H.
Scarborough, Ontario

Addressing the Wound

May 2008

When I was a little boy, I had two major nightmares: one was of a polar bear coming up the driveway and into the house to eat me, and the other was of a Tyrannosaurus rex looking in my window and then attacking me.

Both monsters were as scary as my dad. As a kid, he molested me and woke me up with beatings—tearing me out of bed, screaming and hitting—all while he was drunk. He would come home at three in the morning, drunk and mean, and terrorize me, calling me names and making me do household chores.

I hated him and he hated me. I became a sullen and rebellious child. I was never the son that he wanted. He wanted the all-American jock, but what he got was a brainy, nerdy, sissy-boy. I was an odd child, like a giraffe being raised by a family of deer.

To stuff my anger, to forget my feelings of aloneness, to cope with being "odd" (actually, I was gay but had no idea what was going on), I started stealing pills from my mom, smoking, overeating, and, drinking whenever I could. The year I was sixteen, on Christmas Eve, while the family was at Midnight Mass, my best friend and I got drunk on creme de menthe and cola. I blacked out, broke a bottle of wine, and got blood everywhere. I urinated on the sofa. I was in heaven!

About a year later, I got into a fight with my dad while he was beating me, my mom, and my sisters. It was so violent that the police were called, and they escorted me off the premises. Me!

I was on my own. I drank whenever I wanted and used whatever I wanted. I managed to live that way for fifteen years. By age thirty-two, I was homeless, sleeping on my sister's sofa, and planning my suicide. At the time, I was only drinking two drinks a night—they were 20 oz. tumblers of gin on the rocks with no mixer, but I only had two, so I wasn't an alcoholic like my dad. But instead of killing myself that night, I went to bed with the idea that I would go through with it the next day if things weren't better.

The next morning, a thought crossed my mind: "I'm an alcoholic. I need to go to AA." So I called the AA phone number in my area, and told them I wanted to go to a meeting. I decided to be difficult, and said I needed to go to a gay meeting. I was thinking that maybe there weren't any and I could go on drinking. The woman said there were four that day in my area. I couldn't stump her, so I took the information and went. I stayed sober that day, and the day after the meeting, and I'm still sober, nineteen years later.

About nine months into my sobriety, I was doing the Fourth Step and I wrote down every bad thing that my dad had ever done to me. My sponsor had the nerve to tell me to go through the list and write down my part in every one of those instances. My initial response to most everything my sponsor suggested was "Hell, no!"

Then I would think about what she had asked me to do, talk myself into giving her suggestions a try, and darn if those suggestions didn't turn out to be the exact thing I needed to do.

I went through the list. He hit me ... after I smart-mouthed him. He woke me up in the middle of the night, beat me, and made me water the front yard ... after he had asked me to water it and I'd spent the day playing with my friends instead. He slapped me ... after I'd said no in a mocking tone of voice. It was not a fun inventory.

Did he do horrible things that I had no part in causing? Yes. Was he mean and hateful and violent? Yes. Did he hurt and scar me? Yes. Can I change any of this? No. Was I difficult and rebellious? Yes. Was I lazy and self-centered? Yes. Did I steal from him? Yes. Can I change any of this? Yes.

At the time, he lived about fifteen miles away from me, but there was no way I could have gone there and had a conversation about this stuff without creating more resentment. Also, I could never have expressed my thoughts clearly, because anger and fear would have stopped me from saying everything I needed to say. So I wrote an amends letter.

He called me after he received the letter, and we spoke for about a half hour on the phone. In my entire life (thirty-four years at that point) my dad never said anything to me on the phone except, "Let me get your mother." So talking for half an hour was unheralded, truly overwhelming, and deeply moving for me. He forgave me for all I had done. He accepted my amends and agreed to my modest repayment plan for the money I had stolen from him. Then he said I was right—that things weren't good when we were younger and he drank too much. He didn't remember a lot of what happened, but said he was sorry for hurting me. He let me know he loved me. He cried and I cried.

I wish I could say we became best friends, but we didn't. We never had a close relationship—I never trusted him not to hurt me. He was human. Several times after the amends conversation, he said and did hurtful and hateful things. But we were changed men. We were never the same enemies again. We were family.

Four years ago, I was with him and my mother on the morning he died. I held his hand, and promised to help care for my mother so he could go peacefully. Mom lives with me now, as I promised.

Working the Steps and cleaning up my side of the street helped me. Although I could never forget the terrible things that happened, I could stop reliving them. I was able to stop tearing open old wounds with my resentments and hate. I can move on with a new life. I am at peace today with all that happened. Forgiveness has healed my soul.

Anonymous

A Core of Love

October 2007

I'm submitting my story because I have heard some controversy surrounding the issue of religion vs. spirituality within the program. I am an agnostic who loves AA. I wasn't always an agnostic. I am a product of a very religious family. My education was provided by private religious institutions.

As a child, I simply believed what I was taught, so of course I believed in God. At about the time of puberty, I started to have doubts. I couldn't live up to the standards required to "live in the state of grace"—mostly in regard to sexual thought and conduct. So, the odds were that I would spend eternity in hell after I died. I couldn't see the logic in a God who would bring us into existence only to have a fair percentage of us end up in hell. I became an atheist before I graduated from high school. I can now say, God bless those who believe and live by their religious beliefs. I could not.

When I came to AA, I was past forty years old. I had lived my entire adult life sure in my conviction that there was no God. I liked the people in AA and they told my story when they talked about themselves so I knew I was in the right place, doing the right thing. I figured I could ignore the "God part of the program" and just do the rest. But after being "sober" for a few months and having gotten over the false euphoria of believing that all I had to do was go to meetings twice a week and not drink, I hit a crisis. I became miserable. I was full of anxiety and I couldn't sleep. After ten days of this, I considered hospitalizing myself, but I knew they would give me drugs to put me to sleep. I desperately didn't want that to be the answer.

The people I liked and respected the most in AA seemed to want to talk a lot about God in meetings, so I did the unthinkable. I took Step Three. I pictured the little guru in the B.C. comic strip and asked him what I should do. This is the first real prayer I ever said. The answer came back in a different "voice" than the one I usually "hear" when I'm thinking and it simply said, "Just keep doing what you've been doing." Well, for the previous ten days I'd been going to at least one meeting a day, talking to AA people, reading the Big Book, and writing in a journal. The next Step in the Big Book was Step Four. I began Step Four and knew I was going to be okay. I was able to sleep again.

There is a Higher Power. For me, this is not a theory. I know for sure that at my core is a source of moral guidance, love, wisdom, and energy that, up to the moment before I took the Third Step, I didn't know existed. It has kept me sober, pulled me through some tough times, and produced moments of indescribable joy for over eighteen years. I now believe that there is a spirit in every living thing that wants it to grow and thrive, while other forces, like age, disease, injury, and immorality, work toward deterioration. I call this spirit "God" when I speak at meetings. But if queried to describe the God of my understanding, my answer would be that I do not believe in a "Lord" and I don't know or care if there is life after death. To some, that would make me an agnostic. But I would add that my belief in the God of my understanding gives me a better life here on earth. I am genuinely happy for you if your religious beliefs do the same. Live and let live applies well here. Religious and agnostic alike love Alcoholics Anonymous. It is proof that the program is spiritual and not a religion—and it does not interfere with religious or agnostic beliefs. It just lets us recover from alcoholism's misery and be well.

Carmen C.
Port St. John, Florida

The Transformation

October 2004

W hen did you have your spiritual awakening?" a woman asked me at the end of an afternoon meeting in another town. "I'm eight months sober and I don't think I'm ever going to get it."

I had been immersed in the Fellowship for four years and I didn't have an answer. An avowed atheist, I mumbled something cute like, "You'll have to ask someone older than I!" That seemed to give her hope, but it was I who was unsettled by my own evasive answer.

Was a spiritual awakening necessary for lifelong sobriety? If I didn't have one, was I going to drink again? I thought of all the stuff I was involved in—sponsoring a new woman, editing an AA newsletter, going to the jail meeting every Saturday morning, and being the GSR for my home group. Was I just whistling in the dark until the inevitable occurred? My neat little home filled with teenagers who were just beginning to trust their sober mother—were they all at risk if some manifestation of a God didn't happen to me? Was this empathy for other drunks and tolerance for the world in general all part of my mind's big con job to lull me into false security? As our AA carload headed home that night, happy and noisy and loving life without booze, I felt restless.

Among the books we had in the car was *As Bill Sees It*. I checked, and found sixteen references under the "Spiritual Awakening" heading, and another twenty-one listed under "Spiritual Living." I determined to read them all if I had to, in order to find an answer to my question.

The first reading was Bill's account of his white light experience. I gritted my teeth and quickly went on to the second. It seemed to indicate that awakening was an ongoing thing. Could it be? The next one told me that the spiritually awakened person was in a very real sense transformed. I got excited, for if ever a drunk was transformed—from barroom brawler to PTA mother, from people-hater to lover of drunks—it was I.

The fourth entry is forever imprinted in my sober memory. It told the story of a guy who shared his life freely with others, and then said he didn't have the "spiritual angle" yet. It said it was apparent to everyone else present that he had "received a great gift, and that this gift was all out of proportion to anything that may be expected from simple AA participation," and that the rest of the group felt he was reeking with spirituality. He just didn't know it yet!

I didn't have to read on. I now knew about my own spiritual awakening. It was when I took the first new woman to a meeting and when I went to the jail on Saturday morning instead of sleeping in. A spiritual awakening happened as I left the dinner table in a rainstorm to go on a Twelfth-Step call and again when I said, "Yes, I'll be your sponsor and we'll go through the book together." It began when immeasurable grace was bestowed on me, and continued as I realized that I could never repay what was given to me by the Fellowship.

A spiritual awakening was happening at that very moment as I sat in the car, letting tears of joy run down my cheeks, unashamed in front of my AA peers. I was certain that untold awakenings were in store for me as I trudged AA's Road of Happy Destiny. It's been thirty years since then, and I was oh, so right.

Judith N.
Marysville, Washington

An HP for the Present

July 2007

One of the things I struggled with when I came into AA was relating to the use of the word "God" throughout the Big Book and the Twelve Steps. I was raised Catholic, so there was a God in my life. I had been taught the Lord's Prayer, the Apostle's Creed, and the Hail Mary, so there was prayer in my life, too. But it wasn't working for me.

I wanted what my sponsor had. She told me that I had to pray and surrender my will and my life, daily, over to God. God, a.k.a., a Power Greater than Myself, a Higher Power, God as We Understood Him, Good Orderly Direction, or Group of Drunks. Even with all of these options of God to choose from, I found it very difficult. I am a visual person. I learn visually. I relate to people visually. And I could not visualize any of those things that were being called "God."

When I tried, the God of my childhood kept creeping in. I had a hard time relating to the God of my childhood, a God who said that I was born bad. I had also seen how, throughout history, people had seemed to use that image of God to justify rape, murder, torture, and other atrocities. How could I believe in a God who was all powerful but would let people do horrendous things in his name? And prayer, well, I knew how to say the prayers; I'd memorized them. They had been drilled into me since the first grade. I said them but they didn't mean anything to me. The Lord's Prayer at the end of every meeting meant nothing to me. I got more from holding someone's hand and feeling part of a group made of individuals just like me than I did from saying the prayer.

My sponsor suggested that I try talking to God, so I gave that a shot. But when I talk to someone, I need a picture, in my mind, of who I'm talking to. The only visualization I came up with was the picture on the cover of my Children's Book of Bible Stories that I had received for my First Communion. It was an old man with a long, flowing white beard, white hair, bright blue eyes, and a gentle smile. He stood on a cloud with a staff in hand.

As a forty-year-old mother of three teenagers, when I tried to talk to that vision of God, I felt pretty stupid. How was that God going to understand all that was going on in my life today? That was the God of children and children's worries, not the unique, serious, important, life-changing worries and concerns of a single mom three months into recovery.

I knew I needed to get rid of that picture of God and replace it with something truly greater than myself. In my own, ego-centered way, the only thing that I could visualize as greater than myself was the whole of the universe. I could manipulate and create a lot of different situations, but I knew I could not create the universe and all that was in it. Following that train of thought, if the universe was the only thing greater than me, and there was some unknown presence out there that created the universe, then that unknown presence had to be greater than myself. Also, that unknown presence had to have started with a plan, and had to be pretty smart to make it work. I thought, "Okay, good. Now I have my 'adult' vision of a 'God' that I can work with."

There was only one problem. Whenever I said the Lord's Prayer, or used the word "God" in Big Book prayers such as the Third Step Prayer, the God of my childhood popped back into my brain, and the rest of the prayer became childish and meaningless.

So, being a writer, I decided to rewrite the Lord's Prayer so that I could better relate to it. It said in part: "Creator of the Universe, the Unknowable, the All-Powerful Being, let me do thy will in my life, as decreed by your knowledge. Just for today, give me strength and remove my defects."

My relationship with my Higher Power has grown and matured from that vision of the old, blue-eyed man in white, standing on a cloud, staff in hand. I have a relationship with a Higher Power today because of the suggestions that I followed, whether I thought they were working or not, and the quiet time I spent every day putting in the effort to understand what God meant to me. Today, I am able to talk with God, not just to God. I am able to walk through situations and feelings that, a year ago, I would have drank over. Today, I can let myself relax and know that I am safe—I do not have to control everything and everyone around me.

My relationship with God continues to deepen, grow, and mature each time I ask for guidance and surrender my life into God's capable care, knowing, without a doubt, that I am safe and protected.

Andrea J.
Ypsilanti, Michigan

Spiritual Breakthrough

December 1961

"In my Father's house there are many mansions."
John 14:2

W henever I see a picture of Dr. Albert Schweitzer I think of another doctor—our family physician when I was a child. He was the son of German immigrant parents and he had put himself through medical school. He sang a thunderous bass in the choir of his church for forty years. His mustache bristled with good humor; his laugh, on entering the house, was a rumble of reassurance. He could bring down my temperature just by sitting beside my bed and telling stories of his boyhood. When one of us was seriously ill, he would stand quietly in the sick room, the deep furrows of his face relaxed, his shaggy grey head bent. I know now that he was praying. Though he carried an astonishing array of medicines in two bulging leather bags, his chief remedy was love; I suspect that he was really a faith healer with a medical degree. Looking back at the years of my childhood, I can recall only one adult who seemed to have a close, personal, never-failing trust in God: the old doctor.

Certainly, I grew up with no such trust. Church-going never seemed to cushion the "slings and arrows of outrageous fortune" for the members of my family; they lived in constant sick apprehension of the future.

I reached manhood in the age of H. L. Mencken and the self-consciously clever materialists who knew everything about the world, or they knew a college instructor in "science" who knew everything; or some Institute was about to discover Ultimate Truth any day now—they were working on it.

It was an age when masses of people suffered from a psychic vitamin deficiency. We were like bushmen who eat clay because there is some vitally needed element of nourishment which their diet lacks. We didn't eat clay; we drank bathtub gin. Our premise in the Twenties was, "If life has no intrinsic meaning and no ultimate goal, you might as well get drunk and forget your troubles for a while."

In the paralyzed thirties of the Depression there was still no urge to change our basic orientation; political struggle for social justice and adequate relief projects absorbed all our energies.

Came the forties and the world split at the seams with World War II. Then it was that for me materialism split, too. It suddenly seemed illogical—and even worse, naive—to believe that the wonders of the atom had evolved blindly out of chaos. So I began, after a fashion, to believe in God. But a First Cause is a product of reason. I was still, in a sense, starved.

I slogged along, tossing down the Martinis at lunch until this meal stretched out, and catching the 5:10 home became a problem. Eventually it was hard even to make the 11:55.

At last I felt a nudge by some power greater than myself to look up the AA Fellowship before I wound up in an asylum.

Once inside AA I found a glorious diversity of beliefs in what our founders so wisely and flexibly called "the Higher Power." At first, as for us all, sobriety was like a daily miracle, and as the days added together and I became a little more secure, I began to look around me. United as we are by our common disease and the common remedy by which it is arrested, we still tend, roughly, to group ourselves into three columns, all marching in the same direction and all-for-one-and-one-for-all, but three groups nevertheless.

One of these groups consists of people with the unswerving faith of our old family doctor. During the boozing years they may have lost it but they got it back with sobriety in the Fellowship.

Another group contains people still skeptical of theologies. Some of them are like an AA friend of mine whose father, a stern old New England farmer, would cut the blood out of his son's legs with a buggy whip if the boy missed a Christian Endeavor meeting. The son, now happily in AA, once told me, "I'll admit there is something keeping me sober, but I'll be damned if I'm going to call it 'God.'" The people in this category often have, like my friend, a justified loathing of the word "God" as it is associated with hell-fire sermons, thunderous prohibitions and sore bottoms. Others have had a scientific education and would be quite willing to believe in God in any form, on good and sufficient evidence.

For a long time I was in this group. Like the others, I took the group spirit as a Higher Power and stayed sober. I had not been a "last ditch" drunk—I had felt my mind slipping but it had not completely gone. (Incidentally, I have never known a real low-bottom, in extremis case of alcoholism to maintain a rationalist-materialist outlook when he recovered. There may be some, of course, but I haven't met them.)

The third group puzzled me greatly at one time. I was always looking for some flaw in their judgment or their courage. These were people who once had simple faith, had lost it (usually in college), had been materialists for years, and had come back to believing in God, with or without church membership. They and my old doctor would have understood each other perfectly. For all I know, he may have been like them.

But the people in the materialist group in AA cannot grasp in essence either of the other groups' way of thinking. In the Fellowship they learn tolerance and charity and are too tactful to start any real religious arguments unless their opinions are specifically called for. And if this is their way of working the program, well and good. For them, if it works, it is the "best" AA.

At first I was in the rationalist column even though I had been forced to admit a First Cause. And I thought other members were more than a little childish when they spoke of God as if he were an upstairs neighbor, "and them hollerin' to Him out the window." It was an enigma and an annoyance. I stayed sober by keeping close to the group (with only a few slips and sleeping pills once in a while). Then I began desperately trying to apply the tools of logic and reason to "finding God."

I started on a course of reading which covered the sacred books of the five great religions. The more I read the more theology seemed to be an accretion about a central thread of revelation. At the core was the intimate, personal experience of one man, an experience impossible to put into words, as if the person had been raised to a higher dimension than the three dimensions which contain all "common sense" thinking. The structure of doctrine and ritual which any such original experience acquired down the centuries seemed a good home for those who had been brought up in that religion. But not for me.

Now, the people who had left simple faith for materialism and had returned to a belief in an ever-loving and all-wise God—and a parallel world of "the spirit"— reminded me of a character in a play by Mary Ellen Chase. This is the genial Elwood P. Dowd, a polished, warm-hearted man of obvious culture and intelligence, who insists that his constant companion is a six-foot, invisible white rabbit named Harvey. With me, one of the unconscious barriers to a full acceptance of God, I am convinced, was a sneaking fear that my sophisticated materialist friends would consider me another Elwood P. Dowd, an object of mingled fun and pity.

Anxiety, which had been my constant companion during all the drinking years, was still with me. It had been reduced or shoved into the back of the mind by activity in the Fellowship, but it was still there. And always I was haunted by the problem of pain and evil, against which my reason was powerless. I was told over and over that the only answer to it was faith. But how does a rational man, whose habitual mental processes demand evidence as a basis for any belief, acquire such faith?

I was told to pray for it, yet my prayers seemed like words spoken into a telephone after the service has been cut off. And still I stayed sober, upheld by the group spirit. I spoke at meetings after a time and admitted my belief that a Higher Power had led me to AA; but later I would ask myself, "Am I being hypocritical? Do I really believe in God? What kind of God? How much? How often?"

For my belief fluctuated, back and forth. I had a few moments of overwhelming certainty, alternating with long periods of complete disbelief and even longer stretches of honest agnosticism in which I just didn't have an opinion, one way or another. I can see now that I was making one serious mistake in those days by trying to force myself into the column of simple piety in order to get some relief from the tormenting riddle of evil.

I would argue with myself, "Why be so hard-headed and conceited? Sam is an intelligent man and he has the trust. Gwen seems to walk in the light every step she takes. Marty and Pat have their own certainty—a very liberal church. And as for Gene and Suzie, goodness knows they are young sophisticates and have read all the books, about Zen and everything else. They went ahead and had a baby while Gene was out of a job. Some kind of white magic seems to carry them miraculously through all but insuperable difficulties. They seem to have this faith that everyone talks about. But how do I get it?"

I began to associate with people who seemed to have it, hoping it would rub off on me, just as the AA program rubs off on the rebellious alcoholic.

Things began to clear up a little. I thought, "Certainly all these intelligent people cannot be self-deluded. Maybe I am the self-deluded one. But I cannot follow the honesty part of the program and lie to myself that I believe in a warm, loving, personal God when I don't. I'm willing to admit that the religionists are right, or have an equal chance of being right. Maybe it is just silly pride that is keeping me from seeing something which, without the pride, would become clear to me."

The good people of unquestioning faith could not help me here. Never having lost their faith, they had no idea how to tell anybody the way to it. Only the ex-materialists could understand me. Finally one of these, a man of great insight and scholarship, said, "Maybe you have a wrong idea of prayer. There are all kinds. You don't have to go cringing to God like a mongrel dog, expecting a kick. Just say quietly to God, whether you believe in God or not, 'Look here, Boss, if you want me to obey orders you have got to give me some help.' Try it that way. What can you lose?"

Finally I got so desperate in my struggle to solve the riddle of pain, evil and death that I was willing to take his advice. One of the texts from the Bible which always infuriated me was from Matthew, 10:29: "Are not two sparrows sold for a farthing? Yet not one of them will fall to the ground unless your Father wills it." (Moffatt's translation.) I had seen what happens to a sparrow when it fails to notice the approach of a cat, and the question tormented me, "Which side is God on, the sparrow's or the cat's?" Nature, trustingly called "God's world" by the pious, was obviously a process of sudden death on all sides, one species preying on another. Was this the world of love the believers shared with such confidence?

At last I said, "God, I've come to the end of my rope. Reason is useless. If it is true that 'Your eye is on the sparrow'; if all things are taken care of in the end and all is well eventually, for God's sake give me a sign!"

Nothing happened. Or at least, not at that moment.

I had been getting a little ahead financially, trying to dig myself out of the hole the alcoholic years had put me in. Then one of my creditors moved in, deaf to all pleas of reason and common sense and the claims of other creditors. He had the law on his side and he simply cleaned me out. He got his money, and I was flat broke.

The impact of this hit me on a rainy afternoon. For half an hour I simply sat and seethed. In my mind's eye I pictured myself as a Mongol war-lord and the creditor as a prisoner, helpless before me. I inflicted on him all the most ingenious tortures the Mongols ever devised. Then these got too elaborate and I settled—in my waking nightmare—for chopping him up slowly with a Boy Scout ax. Finally a little sanity returned. I stumbled through our Serenity Prayer. It was a magic spell to keep me away from a bar. I decided to go out for a walk.

I was in utter despair as I plodded along, hands deep in the pockets of my topcoat, my shoulders bent under an unbearable burden.

As I passed a bank I saw a policeman friend of mine looking up at the big clock on the wall of the bank building. His face showed signs of distress, and I asked him what the trouble was.

He said, "The sparrows have built a nest up there behind the clock. Just now I heard them scolding and crying. Then I looked down. A couple of baby birds got crowded out of the nest. They were killed by the fall." He pointed out two tiny, naked, pink bodies on the sidewalk. "It's a shame." Shaking his head he turned and walked on.

I stood silent, my eyes closed. My first acquaintance with death came from just such a baby bird. I was a small child and an aunt snatched my hand away from it, saying sharply, "Don't touch it. It's nasty. It's dead!"

All right. I had asked God to show me the meaning of the believer's claim, "His eye is on the sparrow." Then another line, out of my confused reading, came back to me. It was from Meister Eckhart, the great 14th century mystic: "The eye with which I see God is the same eye with which God sees me." In a flash of absolute knowledge I saw that birth and death are one in God.

Beyond and above reason came the realization that all is one and all is alive. The limited perception of the three-dimensional world exploded in a divine certainty—the fall of the sparrow is one with the miracle of the egg. Life is eternal, the everlasting mercy. My ego had dissolved in love when reason had been pushed to its limits and I was in utter desperation—God is the fall of the sparrow; and sweet Jeanne d'Arc, burning in the market place at Rouen; and Gilles de Rais, twisting, repentant, on the gibbet; Nurse Edith Cavell, facing the bullets; and old Wilhelm Hohenzollern, facing the end of pride in the castle of Doorn. All was the everlasting mercy.

Rationalism had served its purpose, for nothing is created without purpose in the divine plan. Had I never changed my views from materialism, that, too, would have been divinely ordered. We cannot see the pattern any more than a single chip of tile can see the pattern of the mosaic of which it is a part. Now I was marching in that third column beside the men of simple faith and the rationalists. But in the Fellowship we are all moving in the same direction. I know, now, that it is impossible for any human will to go against the will of God in the long run. We can experiment with selfishness or wickedness, even. Outside of time the result is God's will: back and forth the children scamper between the cars; the train rolls onward.

Anonymous
New York, New York

I Can't Fly that Kite Today

April 2002

I am forty-nine years old. As far as I can remember, I never drank responsibly. Through college and my early years of marriage, when I drank, I drank to get drunk. My drinking was always to excess and always dangerous.

Like many adult children of alcoholics, I vowed not to become my father. He died a couple of years ago after a life of alcohol abuse. I can never remember a time growing up when I did not see my father either drinking or drunk. Whenever he got plastered, he started picking on me. It affected me and I developed a deep resentment of my dad.

In 1994, after several dry years, a single drink in a Los Angeles hotel turned into four long years of disaster. My career and family were gone. My reputation in the community was shot. Three rehabs did not help. I was at that hopeless state. I had become just like my dad, with one big exception. I was at least open to Alcoholics Anonymous.

I attended meetings on and off, between sprees. There was something blocking real sobriety. After losing another job, I was drunk again and more hopeless than ever.

A man I met at a meeting came to visit me. He sat and talked with me about his experiences. As he heard my story, he said something shocking. He said I was agnostic! Impossible. You see during those dry years, I accomplished a lot. In addition to becoming the vice president of the local affiliate of a national TV network, I also developed my faith. I went to seminary and earned a master's degree in theology and a doctorate in biblical studies.

Agnostic? Never. I had a relationship with God. I read the Old Testament in Hebrew and the New Testament in Greek. How could I be agnostic? Yet as I listened and searched my heart, I knew he was right.

I was agnostic in one sense. I did not believe that a power greater than myself would help me. I had concluded that my alcoholism after so many dry years was a lapse of faith that God would not forgive. I was struggling with the Second Step of our program.

I marvel now when I read "How it Works" in the Big Book. I marvel at the wisdom of including one small word in the explanation of the Second Step. It's a familiar passage,

1. That we were alcoholic and could not manage our own lives
2. That no human power could have relieved our alcoholism
3. That God could and would if he were sought.

God could relieve my alcoholism. I knew that. But I did not believe he would. I was sure I had crossed a line. I was no longer able to appropriate that power to help. But AA stressed that he "would." The original manuscript was even more emphatic: "God can and will!" I was humbled.

My friend pointed out that as I held onto that belief that God "would not" help me, I was showing a kind of spiritual pride. Surely I was worse than any other alcoholic. Surely I was beyond help.

My turning point came when I was, as the Big Book suggests, "convinced." I was convinced that God could and would relieve my alcoholism. I began to take small steps back to that power greater than myself. The first step was to start my day on my knees asking God to keep me sober. It has worked one day at a time.

But my friend pointed out there was a lot more to do. He joined me on his knees as I prayed a Third Step prayer. Then I had to face that Fourth Step and that tremendous resentment toward my dad. That was hard.

With the support and guidance of my friend, who became my closest friend and my sponsor, I set out to deal with resentment, selfishness, and fear. I followed the outline in the Big Book, looking at where and how this resentment toward my dad developed.

I saw that time when I was eight when Dad, a friend, and I were out flying a kite. Dad as usual was drinking. No matter how hard I tried I could not get that kite airborne! My friend, who was much more athletic than I, ran faster and the kite soared. I remember my dad's words, which cut right to my heart and soul: "Sometimes I wish he were my son instead of you." I was crushed. I carried that moment for forty-one years.

The Fourth Step helped me see that moment in a new light. My dad was sick,

sick with the disease of alcoholism. I understood firsthand how alcoholism affects a person and the family. I asked my spiritual father to relieve me of anger toward my dad. The kite incident and others brought so much to the surface—each time I faced resentment and fear.

I did my Fifth Step with my sponsor-friend. I faced fear. The fear that held me tight for all these years was a fear that my dad did not love me. I faced that fear with many tears. It was so consuming I knew that no human power could help. I needed a power greater than myself to help. I needed to ask for that help through the Sixth and Seventh Steps.

I finished my Fifth Step about midnight and set my alarm for 5:00 A.M., when I knew it would be quiet, to review my work and "know God better." It was a tremendous spiritual experience. As I reviewed my resentments and fears, it became clear that as I feared my earthly father did not love me, I also had come to believe that my heavenly father did not love me. I had. Here was the source of that agnosticism. For all these years, I had a conception of God based on a life of fear, a life of resentment. I shed tears again. This time I asked my heavenly father to forgive me and to help me to trust him and know him. Years of heaviness were lifted.

I still begin my day with prayer, and when I feel overwhelmed by events or circumstances, I often find myself whispering a prayer that goes something like this, "Father in heaven, I just can't seem to fly that kite today. Please help me." And my experience, strength, and hope is that he does.

Frank A.
Scranton, Pennsylvania

Spiritual Honesty

April 1985

A s a recovering member of Alcoholics Anonymous and an agnostic, I would like to present a few thoughts on our Fellowship from an agnostic viewpoint.

One thing that makes my own experience unusual is that I came into the program eighteen years ago professing a conventional belief in God and had no problem accepting the essential part God is believed (by the majority of AAs, past and present) to play in recovery. One of my strongest beliefs is and always has been that a successful, happy recovery is achieved through personal changes brought about by working the Twelve Steps.

After many slips, the last only two years ago, I concluded that one important area I had failed in was an unqualified commitment to honesty. One black memory of my past was a bad conduct military discharge for narcotic use, a source of such shame that I had never told anyone about it except my wife. At my next opportunity as a speaker, I included this episode, and with it went all the guilt I had carried for thirty years.

Coming honestly to terms with my agnosticism was slower and more difficult. The first part was admitting that, even though I considered myself a believer, I had really always lacked the quality of genuine and heartfelt faith. My wife and many people I admire most, both in and out of the Fellowship, have a beautiful faith, which I respect. I harmed myself in fifteen years of hypocrisy in the program, proclaiming a belief I did not really hold. Today, admitting I lack faith does me no harm, because it causes me no needless concern; being different, dissenting from views by a majority of my peers, is not a source of guilt.

The next step was a renewal of my commitment to the Twelve recovery Steps, mainly those Steps that refer directly or obliquely to God. In my first home group, so long ago, I discovered a power greater than myself, that power of love and good helps us recover through sharing, accomplishing together what we could never do alone. I am an agnostic because I cannot honestly say that I have ever experienced or felt anything I am willing to accept as proof of God. I do believe in the human soul, above and apart from our physiology and mortality, even though I cannot prove the soul exists. Some will see a contradiction here, but for me it is just another example of being different, nothing more.

The suffering newcomer to our program is looking for a lifeline, a way out of the hell alcoholism has brought him to. Those who have managed to retain their belief in God suddenly find it all beautifully reaffirmed and can have a relatively rapid transition as recovering members. Others can be turned away by being presented with religious, spiritual, or abstract concepts they are unable to accept or relate to. At their first meeting, newcomers will probably be invited to join in the Serenity Prayer or the Lord's Prayer and will hear a reading of the Twelve Steps. In "How It Works," they will hear how we made a decision to turn our will and our lives over to the care of God as we understood him; how, after a searching and fearless moral inventory, we were ready to have God remove all these defects of character and humbly asked him to remove our shortcomings; how we sought to improve our conscious contact with God, praying only for knowledge of his will for us and the power to carry that out. They may also hear the disclaimer that AA is not a religious organization, but might still get the impression we come fairly close.

I ask that we listen for newcomers who cannot understand or accept the spiritual side of our program, that we stick to the meat-and-potatoes approach and just ask them to try ninety meetings in ninety days with an open mind. We may save a life, for that is what staying or leaving means for many, life or death.

We who are different, whether newcomers or old-timers, need to have the benefit of one of our most important slogans, "Live and Let Live."

W. H.
West Lebanon, New York

Spiritual Honesty
December 2007, from PO Box 1980

Though I had searched my entire life, I never identified with a deity. I tried to accept what others believed, but always felt I was in a masquerade. When I sobered up, I wanted so desperately to have the peace and serenity that I saw on those sober faces that I would have believed in anything.

My solution was to share with my sponsor, then with a trusted friend, then finally, in a meeting. What I shared was this: My personal Higher Power is the collective spirit of humankind—if humans put their heads and hearts together, they can achieve anything.

Blasphemy to some, peace for me. My concern was how my beliefs would affect a young woman who had asked me to sponsor her. I realized that honesty in all things would be my path.

I feel no resentment to the few who try to persuade me that I am lost, or that some particular religious figure is the answer. I love AA and do not feel excluded by others' faiths.

AA brought me sobriety, love, joy, sorrow, and acceptance. More importantly, AA brought me to a true understanding of myself and a power greater than myself—the untiring and persevering spirit of humankind.

Mary E.
Sherman, Texas

Sk8ing Through Life

September 2005

t's a perfect summer Saturday afternoon in midtown Sacramento. The yearning to commune with my skateboard and to get back to what used to be everything to me is pulling me to the converted warehouse that is the closest skate sanctuary from my room at the halfway house on 23rd to the end of B Street on the other side of the railroad tracks down by the American River. Absentmindedly, I readjust the chinstrap on my helmet as I skate along, thinking about the tricks I'm going to try.

The early afternoon light flickers in high through the broad leaves overhead and the wind cools the beading sweat on the back of my neck as I near the railroad tracks. The hairs on my arm stand on end as I realize I'm already putting expectations on my session just by imagining what I want to see happen. I really hate that word, expectations. Alcoholics Anonymous—of which I'm a six month and still counting member—suggests living without them because expectations screw everything up: relationships, sessions, lives, and even perfect summer afternoons in Sac town.

Hmmm. I don't want to ruin my session before I even get there, so I have to let those expectations go. Have to turn 'em over to the Big Kahuna in the sky. Just need to let it flow, have fun, kick back, and watch, because more will always be revealed.

When I arrive at the end of the roughshod road and step into the cavernous yawn of the old warehouse that is the skate cathedral, I am in awe. A ramp has miraculously appeared since my last visit. Six feet tall, twenty-four feet wide, seven-foot extensions, and steel coping make the ramp a tantalizing temptation. I check my helmet strap and jump on. The motion generates a sound something akin to a giant vacuum cleaner on slow-mo. Vhroomm! Vhrooom! with each pass it goes.

Coming off a 50/50, I lose my footing and slam my head against the masonite ramp. Lying on the flat bottom, my head rings as little sparks of light flicker in my peripheral vision like an acid flashback.

I run back up the steep eight-foot transition, drop in, and try again as I shake off the shock of the first slam. I slowly build up speed and then, arming myself with all the self-will I can muster, I drop in, pop off the lip, grab the outside edge of my board, and hold on for dear life. For too long, I hold on. I hold on even though it doesn't feel right. Paying for my willfulness and ignorance of my intuition, I slam hard again. My head is ringing. Stars are flying. My elbows are screaming again in bruised and swollen pain.

This is insane, I think while painfully righting myself from the prone position of the slam. I need to step back and reevaluate my approach because my way just isn't working.

My will got me into AA so why should I try and impose it here? Wallowing in self-pity and watching the other skaters enjoy their session, the definition of insanity that is thrown around the rooms of AA comes to mind. They say insanity is doing the same thing over and over again expecting different results. I figure that I need to do something different.

The late afternoon light and the Delta breeze waft serenely over us and through the park. I'm looking down at the mammoth "U" structure before me. A prayer just might release me from the bondage of fear and of self. This notion, as if by providence, pops into my head. Remembering all those foxhole prayers made during my drunken years of debauchery and self-indulgence causes doubts. This prayer has to be different. Asking God to help me land this trick would be just like all those selfish 9-1-1 prayers I had made when I was out there. I sit for a minute enjoying the breeze while thinking about thinking.

What is my part in this whole affair of self-will run riot? How has fear come to run my thoughts? Rather than trying to do the Big Kahuna's will, I'm trying to impose my own, I realize. It has to be his will, not mine. If I can't pray for what I have, I have to pray for the Big K in the sky to remove my fear. Accepting that it is there is the first step to liberation. "Of course! The Serenity Prayer! How could I be so oblivious?" Closing my eyes, I say it out loud.

"Oh, Big Kahuna in the sky, grant me the serenity to accept the things I cannot change, the courage to change the things I can, and wisdom to know the difference."

Opening my eyes, I see another skater on the opposite deck of the ramp smiling at me. I smile back.

Breathe, relax, trust the process, I say to myself, envisioning the set up for the air before even dropping into the transitions. I have to place the front foot just behind the front truck bolts, position the back foot to pop the tail off the lip, have a good amount of speed, ready the left hand to grasp the outside edge of my board while in the air for a split second, and then let go. It's the last step, releasing the board in mid air, that takes faith. If I do the proper footwork, the aforementioned steps—just as I do in Alcoholics Anonymous with the Twelve Steps of recovery— and have enough velocity, all it would take to pull myself back into the ramp would be the belief, the faith, that it was possible. I have to let to of it completely and trust the process, just as I do in AA.

Instinct and logic tell me to bail out of it when I hit my peak in the air. They scream at me, "You can't just fly through the air like that! What about gravity, huh?" It's counter-intuitive and goes against all logic, that's how I know that it is spiritually the right thing to do. If all I have is a dollar in my pocket and I'm at a meeting, logic tells me to save it for myself for later. If I give it to AA, and have faith in the process, it will come back to me in ways I can't even imagine.

Spirituality is not based on logic, it is faith-driven. Faith makes the impossible possible. Faith has allowed me to be clean and sober for six months. Flying through the air on my skateboard is a test of faith that releases me from the bondage of self, helps me confront my fear, and takes me away from my overly analytical, logical mind.

One more deep breath before I drop in. Vhroomm! Vhroomm! Rolling backward into a tail stall on the opposing wall, I position my feet. Dropping back in, I build speed by crouching low. I'm popping the tail off the lip now, up and over the coping I fly. Grabbing the outside edge of my board, I hit my peak. Now is the moment of truth. I've done all I can at this point. I have to let go and trust in the process: courage instead of fear. Momentarily, I float. Then, the most beautiful sound in the world: all four wheels of my skate touching down on the ramp's smooth surface at the same time. It's a sound of self-assuredness, so satisfying, clean, and true. I'm rolling up the other wall of the ramp now, smiling.

Afterward, the other skater asks me, "Were you praying before you dropped in?"

"Yep. I was," I answer. "It makes me remember why I started skating."

"Cool."

Baxter J.
Sacramento, California

The Sanest I've Ever Been

July 2008

Insanity is doing the same thing over and over and over, but expecting a different result," I said. The other kids stared at me, obviously confused by my answer.

"That's one way to look at it, Erin, but that's not exactly what we're talking about here."

I was in fifth period "Introduction to Psychology" class, and I had just made a total fool of myself. Not that that was uncommon; I habitually showed up to class intoxicated in one way or another, and often said ridiculous things.

My mother entered Alcoholics Anonymous when I was eleven years old, and although every girl supposedly gets words of wisdom and advice from her parents, everything I got was out of the Big Book. Hence, my definition of insanity — one of my mother's favorite AA quotes — was a little different from the one we were discussing in class.

I loved my mother very much, but I had mixed feelings about AA. I didn't see how AA worked in her. Life at home was hard, and she was emotionally abusive. I desperately wanted her love and acceptance, but I wanted her to accept me for what I was: a bright, sensitive, and creative alcoholic and addict. She wanted me to stop being a manipulative, drama-filled, self-pitying alcoholic and addict. Neither of us could accept the other, and I had a hard time believing that AA was a good program if it created psychopaths like her.

I pretended to hate the fact that my mother was never home. "You care more about your stupid meetings than you care about your kids!" I would scream. In reality, every time she left for a meeting, it meant that I had an hour and forty minutes to get high and relax for a while. So, that's what I did. How sweet it was.

The first time I ever had a drink, I wasn't a freshman yet. I was enrolled in "Jump Start," a program at the high school where kids who'd just graduated from junior high could take a high school course over the summer. Four days before it was over, some boys were sipping from a big, glass juice bottle. For some reason, I was drawn to them — they looked like they were having a great time. They told me that there was vodka in the juice.

"Let me get some!" I squealed, and down the hatch it went.

"We better throw this away," one of the boys mumbled, "I don't want to get busted."

But all I could think was, I don't feel anything.

Back in class, the boys still seemed to be having a rollicking good time, whereas I still felt nothing.

"May I be excused?" I asked, raising my hand.

I left the classroom and headed for the trash can where they had thrown the bottle. I sifted through the garbage (smart boys that they were, they'd helpfully covered the drink with crumpled paper and sandwich crusts), and then I grabbed it and drank some more. I stuck the still half-full bottle in my backpack and went back to class.

Within five minutes, we were all caught, suspended, and the liquor was taken away.

This was a rough one to explain to my mom.

"How do you not realize that this is alcoholic drinking?" she yelled, "You dug it out of the garbage!"

I felt nothing except self-pity, because she told me that besides being an alcoholic, I was grounded. I cried, "I'll go to AA! I know you and Dad were alcoholics! I know it's hereditary! I'm sorry! I'll never drink again!" She told me that if I wanted to go to AA I would have to get there on my own, and she would not drive me.

My stepfather dropped me off at an AA meeting, and I was terrified. For the next four years, I didn't touch a drop.

Incidentally, if you ask my mother what happened that day, she says she dropped me off at the meeting, and made me work all twelve Steps in one day.

My mother is a little touched.

Anyway, throughout high school, I refrained from drinking booze, and told people, "I can't drink, because I'm an alcoholic. Got any pills?"

That's right. I knew my limits, and I vowed that for the rest of my life, I was sticking to drugs. And, there were a lot of drugs to be had.

But eventually, I started drinking again, and that's when things really went downhill. When I was seventeen, on my graduation day, my mother requested that I live elsewhere. That was fine with me, although my feelings were hurt. I moved in with my boyfriend's family, started going to college, and got a part-time job with a very large retail chain. Within weeks I was drinking every night until I passed out. My friends and I often stole the alcohol. We had money; we just weren't old enough to buy it. It was the system's fault, not ours.

"Incomprehensible demoralization" is a great way to describe my behavior during those years. I overdosed, cut myself with kitchen knives, and hurt, irritated, and embarrassed all of my friends, over and over and over. One time I got stoned on dog tranquilizers, pulled my pants down in front of my boss at work, and fell over. That was a blast.

I broke up with my boyfriend and got a new boyfriend — not necessarily in that order. I suddenly found myself with nowhere to live. After drinking for three years, I had become homeless, lost my car, dropped out of school, and lost my job. The job had offered to send me to rehab on the company dime, but I thought, How could they be so rude? Eventually, my new boyfriend moved me into his parents' home.

I was very proud to have found a new job, and to have learned to control my drinking. Who knew that two bottles of wine and a six-pack would be socially acceptable? I felt like a new woman, kicking the "hard stuff." The bottom line was, I loved to drink. It was my reason for getting up in the morning; I looked forward to it all day. I loved nothing more than drinking until I passed out. It was all I really knew how to do. Alcohol became my definition.

My boyfriend ended up getting two DUIs and having to go to rehab. I was devastated and cried every night that he was gone. His parents were very loving and let me stay with them, rent-free, even though he was away.

One night, he called.

"Erin, what do you think about this whole rehab thing? I think we should actually try it."

I was furious. The thought of not drinking was like the thought of not breathing. I never denied being an alcoholic; I knew what

I was from day one, and so did he. I put it all out there on the table and now he expected me to change? However, through my anger

I could see that I did love him, so I snapped, "Fine. You're in there for three months, so I'll quit the day you come home!"

Unfortunately, the seed had been planted. For whatever reason, drinking was not fun anymore.

All of a sudden, I wanted to stop drinking, so after a couple nights of drunk-dialing the AA hotline, I finally got to a meeting. As soon as it was over I sped home and downed a few. My boyfriend called me and I told him that I'd gone to a meeting and was quitting drinking ... with beer in hand, of course.

The next morning I felt horribly guilty. Throughout the day, I told a bunch of people that I had quit drinking. I was visiting my friend at the job I had gotten fired from, and I told her that I had quit. But, alcohol was still all I could think about. A young guy came out back to smoke a cigarette on his break, and he was drinking an energy drink. I immediately asked him if he had ever tried a certain type of energy drink that had booze in it.

"Nope, I haven't seen that one," he said.

I felt like I was losing my mind! I didn't want to drink, but I was obsessed!

That night, I was heading home in tears, knowing that I did not want a beer, but that I couldn't get home fast enough to have one. As I drove, I remembered that at that one meeting I went to, they mentioned a 10 o'clock meeting on Thursday nights.

"What day is it? What day is it? Oh my God, please let it be Thursday!"

It was, but I was already fifteen minutes late. I screeched my car in a U-turn and headed for the meeting place. It was a candlelight meeting and I felt so grateful to be there. I didn't want it to end. I was fearful of what I would do when I got home.

As I was heading out the door, I felt a tap on my shoulder and heard a voice say, "Hey, aren't you the girl from outside my work today?"

It was the energy drink guy.

I burst into tears and collapsed right there. I couldn't believe it. He introduced me to his sponsor, who told me to go to the meeting the next night so I could meet his wife, because I needed a sponsor, too.

Somehow, that night, I didn't drink, and I haven't for fourteen months. The candlelight meeting man's wife agreed to be my sponsor and I burst into tears when I met her, too.

It wasn't that difficult for me to admit that I was an alcoholic, because I had always admitted it, and the fact that my life was unmanageable was apparent.

The hardest parts for me were Steps Two and Three, because I was raised as an atheist.

It took me two days to go from being a complete and utter atheist to having a Higher Power. I believed in karma. I believed in positive and negative energy. I believed in good and bad in the universe.

I started praying to good.

I wrote out my resentments, made a list of people that I owed amends to, and started paying people back for what I had taken from them, financially and emotionally.

This program works, because I really got honest and gave it my all.

I am twenty-two years old and I am going to keep working my program to the best of my ability. It is the sanest that I have ever been.

Erin H.
Concord, California

A Program of Action

March 1989

As an atheist with long-term sobriety in Alcoholics Anonymous, I am occasionally asked how I resolve my atheist philosophies with the program's strong reliance on belief in God's participation in recovery from alcoholism. I have been asked, for example, "How do you work the program when you don't believe in God? Do you just skip the God Steps? What do you turn your life over to? I can see how you could do Step One, and maybe even Two, but how does an atheist do Step Three?" I have asked myself all those questions and many more over the years as I learned how to stay sober within AA.

Perhaps the key to remaining atheist and in AA is that I got permission for some flexibility early in my AA experience. The man who urged me into AA told me the other members would speak about God, but I could overlook that and listen to their advice on daily living. He said I could accept their friendship and assistance without buying all their ideas. The woman who took me to my first meeting told me to accept what would help me and reject what didn't—I could choose. She pointed out that chapter five in the Big Book says the Steps are "suggested," which implies the right to reject some of the directives.

Although I was given the permission for selection of ideas, I was also told by my early sponsors that the Steps and recovery go together. In other words, it would probably be necessary for me to find a way to incorporate into my life all the actions described in the Steps. I would reduce the likelihood of gaining a successful and happy sobriety if I simply omitted the Steps that refer to God. So, with the permission for flexibility, I also got the responsibility to find ways to view each of the Steps as compatible with my lack of belief in God. My job would be to interpret the program so I could live with it, literally.

I cannot say when I began thinking about AA's Steps and how I could apply them to my life. I know that my initial sobriety consisted of little more than not drinking and going to lots of meetings. When I did start, to listen to others' advice to incorporate the suggested Steps into my decisions, Step Three seemed the most important one to address. First, that Step contains an absolute declaration for belief in God, and I recognized that reconciling my atheism with such a seemingly incompatible concept might very well determine whether I could remain in AA. Second, everyone told me they had gotten the most benefit from applying Step Three. And third, I kept hearing people say that Step Three was their stumbling block. If that were true for believers, I thought I was facing one heap of trouble. I have since realized I couldn't have been more mistaken—Step Three has been no more difficult than those which have nothing to do with God.

Step Three had been thrust at me almost immediately. It seemed that nearly every discussion meeting I attended during the first few weeks used Step Three as a topic. What a greeting for an atheist! If I had not been so desperate I might also have been too narrow-minded and arrogant to think I could learn anything from all those strong believers. Luckily, I was frightened, miserable, lonely, physically weak, and unable to argue about anything. Because I wanted and needed the safety of AA, I was forced to listen to dozens of people describe their experiences with turning it over, letting go and letting God, and trusting in higher powers. I stuck around because I had nowhere else to go. I didn't do anything about Step Three, of course, but I did find out that all that God talk had not injured me.

My approach to Step Three started with the willingness to listen to spiritual and religious perspectives I had dismissed many years earlier. I did not listen with the intent or hope to convert to a belief in God. I listened because I figured that each Step had a purpose for being and a route for acquiring some aspect of sober, sane living; I needed to find out just exactly what Step Three was meant to do and how I could achieve the purpose. Based mostly on what I heard from others about the effect of the Step, I decided its purpose must be to relieve self-generated conflict and fear. The method almost certainly is to relinquish the compulsive need to control and to do what is reasonable.

Having realized Step Three's purpose, I have spent the past sixteen years trying to hear what people do when they say they turn their will and life over to the care of God. The distinction between what people do and how they talk about and think about that action is very important for me. Someone would tell their method of doing Step Three and it would strike me that I could do that; I could do it without believing in God. I could not, however, think about my action as having anything to do with God as my friend might, because I do not recognize any form of God.

All of us in AA have heard many different methods of acting out belief. Most of the time the process of exercising belief seems to consist of an internal pep talk and then going about one's business. One woman said that she "turns it over" by repeating an old phrase: Hope for the best, expect the worst, and take what comes. And then she cleans house or goes to work or visits a friend or whatever else occupies normal living. She does what actually is the only reasonable thing she can do. I can do the same thing—repeat her phrase to remind me of the reality of chance and the absurdity of expecting to be able to control all aspects of my life, and then go about the business of living.

Another member described Step Three as "going with the flow" of life. That advice helped me try to fit myself to circumstances rather than insist on creating them. They are words for helping me establish more rational views of my role in life's events.

Countless numbers of people have told me they recite the Serenity Prayer as a tool for engendering an attitude of turning it over. I now regard the statements in that prayer, except for the part about asking it to be a grant from God, as a description of a completely sensible way to approach life. Even atheists can learn to recognize the futility of nonacceptance, the value of risking changes, and the way to tell the difference between things we can affect and those we can't. When I begin to worry about things I can do nothing about, I tell myself to "accept what you can't change." Often I have used the ideas in the Serenity Prayer as a trigger for relinquishing my need to control and as a reminder to take action when some discontentment can be remedied.

I find I actually do very little that is different from the actions of those who believe in God. I just think about the actions in a different way. The words of the Serenity Prayer are a concise way to tell myself to do what makes sense because sane and sensible action has a track record of success. When I make a decision to quit trying to control, I do not expect anyone or anything will oversee events and take care of me. I make the decision because it is the reasonable action to take. I get relief from anxieties and fears the same way the believers do—I stop concentrating on what dismays me and direct my attention to activities that are productive. For the past year or so I have been using a Zen observation as a guide to Step Three practice. The Zen master noted that peace and enlightenment come when you stop evaluating in terms of good or bad and merely accept all of life as what is and try to learn from it. No mention of God is there, but that idea conveys a non-combative principle that is quite similar to that of Step

Three and it is said in a way I understand.

Observing what people do, rather than simply listening to how they talk, has been crucial to my interpretation of all the Twelve Steps. Concentrating on discerning the action each person takes allows me to get around the words about God that get in the way of my understanding how various Steps work. Steps work the same way for me as for someone who believes in God. Only the words get changed. My Step Three would say, "Made a decision to turn our will and our lives over to the care of reasonable action."

J. L.
El Granada, California

Now I Have a Choice!

May 1984

The most wonderful wonderful privilege I have in my life today is choice. I didn't know until I came to Alcoholics Anonymous that I had a choice about drinking. I discovered not only that I could choose not to drink, but also that I have choices about most things in my life today. It often seems that things are forced upon me. But if I stop to consider all the facts, I find that there is a range of options available to me. That range is limited only by my attitude, the attitude that says if I can't have what I want now, nuts to it all!

The attitude I have today is also a matter of choice. If I choose to look at the worst possible aspect of any situation, I feel backed up against the wall. I want to scream, yell, and fight in rage; then, with typical alcoholic extremism, I want to give up and feel sorry for myself.

I even have a choice about the way I feel. I can sit and wallow in self-pity, or I can say: "This is the way it is. These are the facts. Now, what can I do about these facts? Do I need to feel this way? How else can I feel about this? What is it that's so terrible here? What is the worst that's going to happen? Do I have control over what's going to happen? How do I even know the worst is going to happen?"

That line of questioning, if answered honestly, usually tells me that I am not living in today. More often, my sponsor tells me that I am not living in today because that idea is much too simple for a complex, sophisticated alcoholic like me to remember on an ongoing, daily basis.

Having gotten back into living in today, I can deal with the feelings I have today. So I feel hurt, injured, resentful? I can choose to wallow in my pain and drag myself around bemoaning my ill fate and the injury to my oh so purely motivated heart: "Ah, I just want to die!" But wait! I don't really want to die. In fact, I have a lot of things I want to do yet. There never to be enough time to do them.

So why don't I start now, instead of hanging around the house wallowing?

Ego: "Don't wanna do anything."

Superego: "Just wanna wallow, huh?"

Ego: "Yup."

Superego: "Well, it's your choice!"

Ego: "Right."

And there it is. Very simple. I don't need to do anything spectacular. Just doing anything at all is a start. I can call a friend and go for a visit. Better still, I can phone the AA intergroup office and ask them to send me the next wet one that calls to be twelfth-stepped. That's sure to give me a lift. Or I can simply go for a walk and breathe the air and be grateful that I am alive and healthy and breathing sober breaths today. So much for the feeling that I'm dy-y-ying.

Well, that's fine for a small depression or a bad love affair. But then, you see, I feel I have no choice about getting up in the morning to go to work to that dreadful, high-pressure job I seem to be stuck in. Well, where along the line did I choose to fund the large mortgage, the expensive vacations, and my so-called trendy life-style? Perhaps those, too, were my choices. Perhaps those things have tied me to that job about which I to have no choice because I have to fund all these "vital" things. Hm-m-m.

If I simply boil my choices down and do not clutter up the facts with rationalizations, I can choose to accept, to confront and negotiate (with myself or others), or to withdraw. (See the Serenity Prayer.) Now, withdrawing may be difficult, especially if I would rather stick around in order to make another person understand my point of view or the validity of my complaint—or if I want to stick around, say, in order to get even. Those are not small things to give up. But I can withdraw. It's my choice!

I can choose to carry the weight of the world and my problems around on my shoulders, or I can turn them all over to my Higher Power and let her worry about them. I choose to pray to Our Mother instead of Our Father. I'm certain both concepts can peacefully coexist in our program. It's our choice. You don't want to talk to any invisible entity, you say? That God bit gets you down? Well, that's your choice. But my Higher Power tells me that I can choose to bang my head against the wall or I can give up and go with the flow. I can choose to be sober and grateful today. It's entirely my choice.

N. S.
Toronto, Ontario

If You Don't like It, You Can Love It!

July 1963

I wonder how many of the ills I see in today's world have answers right in my own heart I could dig out with AA's tools. Using simply our Steps and Traditions, I've had a good share of God's Grace in arriving at some answers lately that help me feel I'm doing my part to light the candles instead of damning the dark.

For me it began when I wanted to free myself of some resentments, our No. 1 offender, that made me uncomfortable. I turned to *Alcoholics Anonymous* and read again its description of how the first AA members went about making "a fearless and searching moral inventory" of themselves, not of other people.

Their suggestion of writing down a "grudge list" seemed a practical, easy way to start. But I was disconcerted to find on my list mostly AA members' names!

This shouldn't have been too surprising, since I have close relations with far more AA members than with civilians. But when I traced the reasons behind the grudges, it was sad to see how much fear is still involved after some years in AA. I had let my ego get big and swollen again, and naturally that's where I got hurt.

Reflection showed that I tend to have grudges against people whose opinions differ from mine because I fear that my opinion—an extension of my ego—will not prevail.

For example, my list showed that I had resentments against fellow members who were, it seemed to me, intolerant of rich mink-clad drunks, or young alcoholics, or Jewish members, or ex-convicts, or women members, or Negro alcoholics, or members on slips, or members who had been helped by drugs, or members who praised psychotherapy, or members who professed to be agnostics, or members who worked in non-AA fields of alcoholism, or doctors who are ignorant of alcoholism. Let me set that straight: my grudges were against my fellow members who were intolerant of any of the above.

In all, I counted twelve intolerances in other members—until I suddenly saw I had titled the page, "My Grudge List." There it was in writing—my own private list of a full dozen intolerances that were mine, not those of anybody else. Why did this load of resentments, or prejudices, trouble me?

To be safe I decided to follow directions. I applied Step Five to my wrongs of thinking, and went on to Six and Seven with them. Since then, Ten and Eleven have helped me keep my prejudices against other members' (and even non-members') attitudes under control much better. So far it's just miniature progress, but that's the way toward achievement.

The more I ponder the lessons of love for, and service to, all human beings in our Traditions One, Two, Three and Twelve, the stronger I become in the struggle to rid my life and heart of intolerance, and the freer I become to carry out God's will for me. His plan, as I understand it, doesn't seem to have any shred of prejudice, or bias, or intolerance, or resentment in it. I've even learned a new fount of blessings is located in the things other members do which I'm tempted to label angrily, "not good AA." But I have to search out the good; it's quieter than the bad.

Earlier I said that maybe our program offers answers to other problems of the world. Here's one experience: I find myself now much less bitter and defiant toward the Russian people. I'm not for Communism, but at least I don't have to poison my heart any more with hatred of people who are. For far too long I have let damning labels, quickly applied on too little evidence, ruin my life.

Now I find I can do much more work for the causes I believe in because I don't have to fight so emotionally, or hate anybody while doing it. If views other than mine prevail, that may be God's will for somebody, too.

Not long ago a fairly new Negro member led my group's closed discussion meeting. "I'm a Negro, reared in the South," he said. "Think for a minute of what that means."

We waited silently. We are an almost all-white group.

"Through the grace of God, AA has helped me get over hating white people," he said softly. "In AA I have learned the meaning of friendship without color. I can actually love all of you now. I have to, to stay sober."

I knew what he meant.

Anonymous

Manhattan, New York

THE TWELVE STEPS

1. We admitted we were powerless over alcohol—that our lives had become unmanageable.

2. Came to believe that a Power greater than ourselves could restore us to sanity.

3. Made a decision to turn our will and our lives over to the care of God as we understood Him.

4. Made a searching and fearless moral inventory of ourselves.

5. Admitted to God, to ourselves, and to another human being the exact nature of our wrongs.

6. Were entirely ready to have God remove all these defects of character.

7. Humbly asked Him to remove our shortcomings.

8. Made a list of all persons we had harmed, and became willing to make amends to them all.

9. Made direct amends to such people wherever possible, except when to do so would injure them or others.

10. Continued to take personal inventory and when we were wrong promptly admitted it.

11. Sought through prayer and meditation to improve our conscious contact with God as we understood Him, praying only for knowledge of His will for us and the power to carry that out.

12. Having had a spiritual awakening as the result of these steps, we tried to carry this message to alcoholics, and to practice these principles in all our affairs.

THE TWELVE TRADITIONS

1. Our common welfare should come first; personal recovery depends upon A.A. unity.

2. For our group purpose there is but one ultimate authority—a loving God as He may express Himself in our group conscience. Our leaders are but trusted servants; they do not govern.

3. The only requirement for A.A. membership is a desire to stop drinking.

4. Each group should be autonomous except in matters affecting other groups or A.A. as a whole.

5. Each group has but one primary purpose—to carry its message to the alcoholic who still suffers.

6. An A.A. group ought never endorse, finance or lend the A.A. name to any related facility or outside enterprise, lest problems of money, property, and prestige divert us from our primary purpose.

7. Every A.A. group ought to be fully self-supporting, declining outside contributions.

8. Alcoholics Anonymous should remain forever nonprofessional, but our service centers may employ special workers.

9. A.A., as such, ought never be organized; but we may create service boards or committees directly responsible to those they serve.

10. Alcoholics Anonymous has no opinion on outside issues; hence the A.A. name ought never be drawn into public controversy.

11. Our public relations policy is based on attraction rather than promotion; we need always maintain personal anonymity at the level of press, radio and films.

12. Anonymity is the spiritual foundation of all our traditions, ever reminding us to place principles before personalities.

AA Grapevine

AA Grapevine is AA's international monthly journal, published continuously since its first issue in June 1944. The AA pamphlet on AA Grapevine describes its scope and purpose this way: "As an integral part of Alcoholics Anonymous since 1944, the Grapevine publishes articles that reflect the full diversity of experience and thought found within the A.A. Fellowship, as does La Viña, the bimonthly Spanish-language magazine, first published in 1996. No one viewpoint or philosophy dominates their pages, and in determining content, the editorial staff relies on the principles of the Twelve Traditions."

In addition to magazines, AA Grapevine, Inc. also produces an app, books, eBooks, audiobooks and other items. It also offers a Grapevine Online subscription, which includes: new stories weekly, AudioGrapevine (the audio version of the magazine), the Grapevine Story Archive and the current issue of Grapevine and La Viña in HTML format. For more information on AA Grapevine, or to subscribe to any of these, please visit the magazine's website at www.aagrapevine.org or write to:

AA Grapevine, Inc.
475 Riverside Drive
New York, NY 10115

Alcoholics Anonymous

AA's program of recovery is fully set forth in its basic text, *Alcoholics Anonymous* (commonly known as the Big Book), now in its Fourth Edition, as well as in *Twelve Steps and Twelve Traditions, Living Sober,* and other books. Information on AA can also be found on AA's website at www.aa.org, or by writing to:

Alcoholics Anonymous
Box 459
Grand Central Station
New York, NY 10163

For local resources, check your local telephone directory under "Alcoholics Anonymous." Four pamphlets, "This is A.A.," "Is A.A. For You?," "44 Questions," and "A Newcomer Asks" are also available from AA.